T0195593

The Wedding, the Wine, & the Water

MARY T. BILLINGS

WESTBOW
PRESS®
A DIVISION OF THOMAS NELSON
& ZONDERVAN

The Holy Bible, English Standard Version® (ESV®)
Copyright © 2001 by Crossway,
a publishing ministry of Good News Publishers.
All rights reserved.
ESV Text Edition: 2016

Scripture taken from the King James Version of the Bible

Scripture quotations marked (NIV) are taken from the Holy Bible, New International Version®,
NIV®. Copyright © 1973, 1978, 1984, 2011 by Biblica, Inc.™ Used by permission of Zondervan.
All rights reserved worldwide. www.zondervan.com The "NIV" and "New International Version"
are trademarks registered in the United States Patent and Trademark Office by Biblica, Inc.™

WestBow Press books may be ordered through booksellers or by contacting:

WestBow Press
A Division of Thomas Nelson & Zondervan
1663 Liberty Drive
Bloomington, IN 47403
www.westbowpress.com
1 (866) 928-1240

ISBN: 978-1-9736-2297-0 (sc)
ISBN: 978-1-9736-2298-7 (hc)
ISBN: 978-1-9736-2296-3 (e)

Library of Congress Control Number: 2018903182

Print information available on the last page.

WestBow Press rev. date: 4/19/2019

Preface

As I read the Wedding of Cana, found in John 2, I was intrigued with the elements – Wedding, Wine and Water. To search out a better understanding I headed to the local library.

Once at the library, I found a book on Jewish Orthodox weddings, and I was moved. In the traditions of this incredible faith, I saw the gospel disguised with symbolism and a prophetic line that led from the Old Testament to the New Testament. I had previously done a study by Beth Moore that included detailed teaching on the Tabernacle which also fed my interest. I saw many connections between the Jewish marriage traditions and my Christian faith. Notes were scribbled on scraps of paper as I attempted to gather the details. From there, a book began to form. More research at more serious libraries was necessary. More information led me into a deeper understanding of God's plan, the redemption of mankind, and his calling us through the beauty of the wedding covenant.

God is the master of prophetic detail, bringing his plans so beautifully together and using symbolism within the wedding ceremony and throughout the Bible to weave together his plan to pursue us with a tenacious love through his son, Jesus.

I hope you enjoy this book as it moves through the wedding traditions tying into the Word of God. May you be blessed as the Holy Spirit leads you to a fuller knowledge of his delirious love for you and his plan for you as his future bride.

Blessings,

Mary T. Billings

Introduction

Ancient Jewish traditions are vast according to time, place, and culture. My research is painted with broad strokes as I sought to remain objective and, at the same time, not allow the book to be overloaded with too many details.

Though this book uses the traditions of the ancient Jewish wedding as a vehicle to move through the gospel, it is not limited to the wedding. American wedding traditions are not forgotten but laid out as a distant relative.

For those of you who do not have a base knowledge of the Jewish traditions, here is a brief explanation of some of the terms used throughout the book.

Erusi: the proposal.

Mikveh-a ritual bath that is an act of spiritual purification.

Huppah-the wedding canopy, symbolic of the groom's home.

Mohar-the bride price.

Ketubah-the marriage document.

Kiddushin-the betrothal, but more legally binding.

Nissuin-the second part of the marriage ceremony that can take place up to a year after the Kiddushin.

Yuchid-the tent where the bride and groom will share time after the wedding ceremony.

Hamotzi-the bread served at the wedding banquet.

Kittel – white robe worn on special occasions

This book is not a historical text, nor should it be used as a reference. My only goal is that you gain an understanding of God's persistent character as it shines through not only his word but also the rich, meaningful wedding traditions. The Wedding of Cana, found in the book of John, Chapter 2, is the inspiration for this work and I hope you find a chance to read it.

Contents

1

The Invitation and the Proposal

"Come Follow Me"
(Mark 1:17a)

A Simple Love Story

It is the beginning of every love story; boy meets girl, and girl notices boy. Shortly after meeting, words are exchanged alongside stolen side glances filled with lingering warmth. Under the shade of a fig tree, they meet and whisper the hopes for their future.

A meeting has been set up by boy, boy's father and girl's father. The men discuss the details of the match, including the bride price: the Mohar, and a marriage contract: the Ketubah. Next, the groom presents his offer to his future bride, he stands in front of her with an old table between them. Alone in the center is a single cup of wine. With his eyes, still on the girl he loves, the boy takes a drink from the cup of wine and offers it to her. Slowly, lowering her eyes as she reaches for the cup, she takes and drinks. Her acceptance comes without hesitation, yet with grace. His father pays the bride price immediately. The groom offers the bride a special gift, something he has carved from the wood of a fig tree. These layers of invitations endear her heart to his. They are now married and set apart for one another.

Immediately the groom departs to head back to his village to begin the work of preparing their home. During this time, the bride and groom exchange letters bridging the gap of separation.

After months of preparation and anticipation, she knows he will be arriving sometime soon. She listens and waits daily for a clue that he is on his way to bring her home. The time is drawing near, she senses it. Wearily waiting one evening, she hears a sound. In the light of the full moon the wind changes direction beaconing her to the bedroom window. She is sure she heard an echo of his voice. Leaning out of the window, she hears singing and the sound of feet running over the pathway leading to her home. Shouts of joy disrupt her patience and the love song surrounds her as she gathers her things with a trembling heart. Her mother and father stand at the bedroom door with quivering smiles that brim with pride. This choice of husband gladdens them. Nurturing whispers are hurried as mother reminds her to pack all her belongings. Watchful with admiration, younger sister gathers around as her mother ties the bridal dress into place and attaches the veil. Father looks on as tears of joy paint his face with tenderness.

With more shouts of jubilation, the groom pounds the front door, calling the bride to receive him. Parents open the door and a young man stands at the doorstep finishing his jubilant love song. Parents deliver the delicate hand of their daughter to his open ready hand. He lifts the veil from her beloved face to confirm that the young woman behind it is indeed his bride. He breaks forth a smile and places the veil over his bride with loving satisfaction. An intimate ceremony takes place immediately. It begins with another shared cup of wine. He hands her a copy of the Ketubah, blessings are spoken over the newlywed couple, and the groom places a ring upon the bride's finger. Now they journey to their new home, a new beginning. Walking backwards with his eyes set on his beloved bride, he leads the way. He is overcome with love songs, the high notes share his promises to her, while the low notes tell of a yearning experienced throughout their separation. Her parents' walking beside her, guiding her future by speaking words of wisdom and reciting psalms of encouragement. The couple arrives. The groom goes in ahead to briefly glance around, assured that all is as perfect as planned. Still singing, eyes set on his lovely bride, the groom leads her into their home for the first time.

They spend time having a savory meal while sharing another cup of wine. During this time, they get to know each other intimately. This is the beginning of their private relationship as husband and wife, leading to a physical expression of their love for one another. Their marriage is now consummated, and they begin the journey of becoming one flesh. Let the celebration begin!

The Beginning of It All

Proposals, engagements, and weddings through time and culture are as diverse, yet similar as one's taste in food, music or literature. If we strip away the culture and era, we are left with the basics; people love to eat, listen to music, and read.

Weddings contain many similar elements; a proposal, an engagement time, and a marriage ceremony or tradition. Further strip away traditions and span of time, you will find consistent elements tying together the entity of marriage with a thread connecting us in this possession of two people brought together into a new beginning called marriage.

The traditions of the Jewish wedding in this book lean towards ancient times, many still known, practiced and revered today. The study of these traditions has torn through the veil of my heart increasing thanksgiving, revealing the deep beauty found in marriage rendering my heart wide open with joy.

When a marriage was arranged in the early Jewish culture, it was set up significantly different from American culture. A single man and his father would travel to the prospective bride's home to meet with her father to discuss the prospect of marriage. At this meeting, they discuss of the bride price: the Mohar, and the details of the marriage contract: the Ketubah. If both parties agree, the bride would be promised, engaged to the groom: the Erusin. Take a step in-time or move geographically, and the bride would be presented with this proposal and its terms. She could either accept or decline. If the invitation to marriage is accepted, the couple are engaged.

In the Jewish culture the proposal can present itself in a more ancient tradition. A table holding a single cup of wine is set between the young man and woman. The young man extends a cup of wine to the young woman and if she accepts the invitation to this marriage, she will demonstrate her acceptance by sharing the cup of wine. This is called the Kiddushin. At this time, they are legally married, yet for approximately the next year they will be set apart for one another. The groom will go home and prepare a place for them to live. Living separate until the wedding ceremony: the Nissuin. Then the marriage will be consummated immediately! Let the celebration begin!

The Invitation Arrives

Through time you have probably heard about the engagement of a certain young couple and are anticipating the save the date and or the invitation to arrive in the mail. The day it arrives, you methodically set the invitation apart from all the junk mail and bills, then with slow motion hands, you carefully open the invitation not to miss the presentation that has been so precisely assembled. Made of the finest quality paper, delicately printed font, edges embossed with flowers, and layers of stacked tissue paper, the invitation is exquisite!

The calendar is marked, planning of gifts and travel arrangements are set, and your curiosity is sparked. The greater the invitation, the higher the expectation!

The bride and groom started their relationship with an invitation. Maybe it was to a formal dinner or a casual coffee date. However it began, it led to the same place. The question is popped, as we Americans say, like it was a can of soda that exploded!

This invitation from the mouth of the groom to be are the words carefully and anxiously chosen, written upon his full heart.

Christ's Invitation

Christ's invitation to "Come follow me" is direct, inviting, and spoken with an intimate urgency. It is a relentless invitation that does not expire but requires only a precondition; our self-realization as a preponderance sinner and a need for a Savior. Because his love is faithful and true, the invitation sits waiting to be opened. He desires and requires your presence at the banquet to celebrate his delirious love for you.

> *As a young man marries a young woman, so will your Builder marry you; as a bridegroom rejoices over his bride, so will your God rejoice over you.*
> *(Isaiah 62:5)*

Do you know this love of God who rejoices over you? Do you know this God who made you so that you can be loved by him? Who fights for you to be his?

We were created with the eye of an artist and the pride of a Father. Made in his image for his purpose. He desires your company. Invited. Loved. Chosen. These words will stand and pursue.

Rebekah
Genesis 24

A story of a proposal that echoes our invitation from Christ.

The story of Rebekah is a perfect story for Once Upon a Time. This is a story we should tell our daughters and granddaughters. This is a story we should allow ourselves to get caught up in. As I think about the meaning of this story, I am reminded how this echoes the call on our lives, wooed by the Holy Spirit, invited and set aside for Christ. He has sent his servant ahead to invite us to become the Bride of Christ.

This is the story of an invitation to marriage. Abraham sent his servant back to his homeland of Ur to find a wife for his son Isaac. God had made a covenant with Abraham promising him countless offspring. Now it was imminent for Isaac, his son, to marry and be part of carrying forth this promise.

*Then the word of the LORD came to him: "This man will
not be your heir, but a son who is your own flesh and blood
will be your heir." He took him outside and said, "Look up at
the sky and count the stars—if indeed you can count them."
Then he said to him, "So shall your offspring be."
(Genesis 15:4-5)*

The servant traveled four hundred miles with ten camels in tow. When
he arrived in Ur, he prayed to God requesting he would recognize the
woman God had chosen to be Isaac's wife. Rebekah appeared just as he
ended his prayer and offered water to the servant's camel with the exact
words the servant used in his prayer. The servant was invited to dine
and stay with her family. However, he refused to eat dinner until he
could share why he came to the land of Ur. Perhaps he began by sharing
stories of Abraham and Sarah, details of the covenant God made with
Abraham, the long-awaited arrival of their son, Isaac, and their many
blessings of great wealth. I imagine Rebekah was beginning to fall in
love with Isaac before she knew what God had planned for her. Then it
became clear, the servant revealed that Rebekah was the chosen wife for
Isaac. Immediately and humbly, she accepted the invitation to follow the
servant and become the wife of Isaac. Rebekah said "yes" to the proposal
of Isaac before meeting him because she believed all the servant told her
about Isaac and his father.

We too believe in the Scriptures and the promises within. We follow Christ
before meeting him face to face. In verse 16 the servant said the girl, Rebekah,
was very beautiful. Well, what about your beauty my friend? Our beauty
comes from knowing Christ. Christ will take our rough edges and make
them smooth. He will take our calloused tongue and sweeten it. He will take
our stone heart and give us a new heart of flesh. He will take our thin skin
and strengthen it with God confidence. Now we are ready to walk the red
carpet. Our joy is in the Lord. His light will radiate in this cold, dark world.
Our hope in Christ is reflected through our countenance. Radiate his love!
As you hear the stories of Jesus and his sacrifice on the cross, his
unconditional love for you and promise of eternal life, how do you
respond? Do you, like Rebekah, fall in love with Jesus as you hear about

God's majesty and how he created you to join him? When you hear his invitation, "Come follow me," do you desire to follow? Or do you hesitate to accept this offer? The invitation to join Christ is immediate, intimate, and has an urgency couched with tenderness. Rebecca did not wait to follow the servant to meet Isaac. She believed all that he said was true and responded with a readiness that blessed her. She married Isaac, and as the end of the chapter states, "she became his wife and he loved her." Her obedience and faith in the servant's call brought her love. God's love is pursuing you. The very essence and being of love wants you to be with him for eternity. Are you going to respond to this invitation of love without hesitation like Rebekah?

Christ Alone

> Jesus answered, "I am the way, the truth and the life. No one comes to the Father except through me."
> (John 14:6)

Christ's invitation is very pointed and clear. To reach the Father, one must go through Jesus. He is the life and the way. He is the vehicle to the Father. He is the truth. All other gods, prophets, and religions promising eternal life are not telling the full truth. There is no darkness in heaven and there is no darkness in knowing Christ. He will come into your life, remove your darkness, and fill it with his light. The story of God's plan and how Jesus is the ultimate answer are written of in the Bible. I encourage you to take it up and read it and start to grasp all Jesus is offering you. So, either you can count on Jesus as the only way, the truth teller, and our giver of life, or you can't. These promises are either real for you and you can have faith and hope in Christ or they aren't true. Are you willing to place your life in his hands?

The gift from God is an undiminishing eternal gift. It is a gift God wrote with the blood Jesus shed on the cross, permanent, not to be revoked. It is "the greatest gift" man can receive. But there is more. When we receive Christ, He gives us a second gift. He sends us the Holy Spirit to comfort us, guide, and fill us with the very breath of God. We are not promised an easy life, but a life filled by the breath and power of the resurrected Lord to sustain, comfort, and encapsulate us with His enduring love.

The Holy Spirit resides in us with love, taking up space in our life through our heart. He will reside in us because we are now his. We have accepted the invitation and he moves in with urgency, quickly taking residence with an abundance of love, and a commitment much like a marriage; to reside with us forever!

> *For God so loved the world that he gave his one and only*
> *Son, that whoever believes in him shall not perish, but have*
> *eternal life.*
> *(John 3:16)*

With Christ in our lives different blessings come to us. Some of them are blessings through obedience. Some come through suffering. And some come by seeking him. The rest are just because: because we are His, because we are now part of His family, because He loves, and because He wants us, to know him deeper.

The Ancient Jewish Wedding Traditions; a Tradition of Compassion.

Let us return to the Jewish Wedding Traditions. This faith has traditions that beautifully demonstrate compassion. One tradition calls for an invitation to the poor and destitute of society. This demonstrates that at the root of their faith are traditions of compassion and grace.

We all are in a condition of poverty. If we are to look at ourselves honestly, we are left with a broken person who does not measure up to what God created us to be. Once you get to know God, then you start to view His holiness. His holiness will reflect into our broken cracks and start to be filled with his grace that was brought by the cross.

An Invitation to the Poor

In the book of Luke, Jesus tells a parable that addresses the tradition of inviting the poor to a banquet. Like many of Jesus' parables, this one relates to the Jewish lifestyle and traditions.

> *Then Jesus said to his host, "When you give a luncheon or dinner, do not invite your friends, your brothers or sisters, your relatives, or your rich neighbors; if you do, they may invite you back and so you will be repaid. But when you give a banquet, invite the poor, the crippled, the lame, the blind, and you will be blessed. Although, they cannot repay you, you will be repaid at the resurrection of the righteous."* (Luke 14:12-14)

Have you invited someone poor, blind, or crippled to your home? Christ is asking us to be generous and to love all. There is a blessing for those of us who invite the unfortunate to celebrate life with us and do not exclude them based on their circumstances. This is the love of God. He considers the heart of the man. We are to have compassion. This is a different list than one we naturally go to when planning a dinner party.

Christ is planning a banquet for us. While heaven is a place of continuous celebration, there is one banquet that is going to welcome us through the gates. I can only imagine all the people of the world, from every race and time, being present. And all of those who suffered physically through blindness, paralysis, or a diminished mental capacity while on earth will be made new. No man will be a stranger to one another. There will be love and joy in everyone's hearts. There will be no walls or borders between the haves and have nots, a new order of things. We will all be brothers and sisters in Christ celebrating with him in the most glorious banquet. This banquet will out shine the dinner of kings and queens. And what do you think the best part is? Jesus wants us there as his honored guest!

When one of those at the table with him heard this, he said to Jesus, "Blessed is the one who will eat at the feast in the kingdom of God…. 'Go out quickly into the streets and alleys of the town and bring in the poor, the crippled, the blind and the lame."
(Luke 14:15-21)

I love the urgency and target of the final invitation! "Go out quickly!" Time is running out! There are so many seats to fill! Let no-one perish! Fill the room with the have nots, the handicapped, the discriminated against, the poor and neglected. Come prisoners! Come prostitutes! Come slaves! Come unmentionables and those listed of ill repute! Come all!

There is room! Heaven does not have a limited capacity like the signs you read on a restaurant wall. All are invited! The book of Ephesians, tells us that God chose us before the foundation of the world. Our invitation is long standing before the earth was made. He desires for us to join him before time was set. His desire is to have his house full. Do you desire to taste, see and attend this banquet? Have you taken time to whisper to this King, and accept his invitation to his royal table?

An Invitation to the Birth of a King

And there were shepherds living out in the fields nearby, keeping watch over their flocks at night. An angel of the Lord appeared to them, and the glory of the Lord shone around them, and they were terrified. But the angel said to them, "Do not be afraid. I bring you good news that will cause great joy for all the people. Today in the town of David a Savior has been born to you; he is the Messiah, the Lord. This will be a sign to you: You will find a baby wrapped in cloths and lying in a manger."

Suddenly a great company of the heavenly host appeared with the angel, praising God and saying, "Glory to God in the highest heaven, and on earth peace to those on whom his favor rests."

When the angels had left them and gone into heaven, the shepherds said to one another, "Let's go to Bethlehem and see this thing that has happened, which the Lord has told us about."
(Luke 2:8-15)

Shepherds play a key role in the Bible. A few examples; the great King David began as a shepherd, multiple Psalms feature the relationship between a shepherd and his flock, and one of Jesus's names is "Our Shepherd". There are many reasons for this emphasis on shepherds throughout the Bible. A shepherd's work usually calls him to be with sheep continually. This means living with them, sleeping beside them, and tending to them around the clock. It usually was an unpaid position assigned to the youngest son of the family. Often, this son would not be in line to inherit the family property. Because of this low social status, a shepherd is not the most likely person one would invite to the birth of a child.

If I had just had a baby, I would not be too thrilled about the smelly condition of these shepherds as they entered the room to visit my newborn child. Bring them some hand sanitizer please! But God is always looking at the heart of a man and not his position or exterior appearance.

Today, if you were invited to see Princess Kate and Prince William's baby, Charlotte, at the hospital after she was born, you would have to be some sort of important person. Probably one of the few select people outside the family circle. You might need to be cleared with a background check, not to mention you would shower, shave, and wear a clean pair of dungarees.

The birth of Jesus is beautiful. There was no pomp and circumstance. He came quietly, with humility, and the poor and lowly were invited. Imagine if you lived in a third world country or in America where we have great poverty and neglect. Somehow you hear the news of how Jesus came quietly, born to poor peasant parents, born as man surrendering his kingship, born in the open air, lowly conditions. Then you hear that he invited the poor, lowly shepherds to visit his birth. Add on to it, he sent a singing telegram of angels, set in the starry night under-lite with one newly created star set out for this special night. The lowly and poor, invited to see the birth of our Savior King. Such a brilliant invitation delivered to those thought to be forgotten, working in a field. Christ's humble birth set no stumbling block to the poor and the lowly. Come all!

His Invitation to the Sick

> On hearing this Jesus said to them, "It is not the healthy who need a doctor, but the sick. I have not come to call the righteous but sinners."
> (Mark 2:17)

> "…Be still, and know that I am God."
> (Psalm 46:10a)

Sin makes us unhealthy and Jesus came to call us out of it to a place of healing. He came for all sins. He invited the drug dealers, the users, abusers, and the detestable. He invited the proud, the intellectuals, the hard of heart, the educated, and the distracted. Have you made your reservation? No reservation denied. No tie required. No special connection of obligation. Just Jesus Christ. No status standing. The only need rendered, acceptance of this personal invitation. In Psalm 46:10 God invites us to be still before him. He invites us to empty our minds and be in his presence. He knows your needs loved one. The words "be still," translate to rest. That is the first prescription for a person who is ill. Through rest we mend, repair our body and mind. Imagine God hovering over us as we rest, stitching us up and mending our broken spirit, our disease-ridden bodies, and our hurting hearts, our addictions! When I learned about the meaning of these words, I thought of a rag doll and how dolls are tattered from wear and tear through time. Sometimes they lose their stuffing, an arm gets pulled out of the socket, or an eye falls off. They are worn out from being loved and dragged around. Years ago when my girls still played with dolls, I took them to a little cottage doll store and we walked around looking at dolls from all over the world and across time. But most interesting was what was happening at the back counter; a doll hospital. Behind the counter, women dressed in white jackets with the title Dr. in front of their name tended to the patients. Young ladies and old lined up, holding their injured broken dolls carefully folded into crocheted blankets. The doctors gingerly asked for the dolls name and what ailed her. Accessing her need, the doll checked into the hospital for a week or so. Imagine the Lord has invited you to quiet yourself before him. He lays you out on His lap like a rag doll while He mends you. He mends your broken heart. Your broken spirit. Your despair. Does He need to replace your stuffing through years of wear? Does He need to sew an eye back on? Does your hair need to be reset? The great physician, Jesus Christ, has invited you into His presence to mend you. As my husband so cleverly said, "He invites us to the gos-pital!" (The gospel plus hospital equals the gos-pital.)

There is no way we can repay Christ for his invitation and the gift of eternal life. We are poor in the flesh. We are poor in our generosity. We are rich in our sinfulness. Yet, he loves us and invites us to have a relationship with him, he gave his life and he keeps giving. He changed us from our fallen wretched state into his bride, whom he rejoices over. He is a God full of grace and mercy!

Chapter 1 Questions

1. What are your thoughts on the comparison of Jesus's invitation to a marriage proposal?

2. Do you believe that God created you for his own purpose to have a relationship with you?

2

The Engagement

An Engagement Party

My daughter asked me to accompany her to a wedding in Nigeria. She was invited to be a bridesmaid of a girlfriend in the states. The bride and groom had previously lived in Nigeria; thus, the wedding took place there. The decision was easy. I love weddings! I love my daughter! And I love to travel!

The day before the wedding was the formal engagement party. This was my personal highlight of the trip. It was performed in their native language, and was rich with tribal traditions and rituals. A generous guest sitting next to me gave a broad translation of what was happening. But truly, without understanding the words, what was being performed was evident of a deep abiding root in the gospel.

As the groom and his groomsmen entered the engagement party, they were met by an adversary blocking further entry. The groom's intent for entering was questioned. Tension escalated and lasted a very long moment as the adversary tried to divert him, arguing against his entrance and claiming of his bride. The bantering persisted back and forth, his love declaration for his bride remained untouchable, relentless, lovingly fierce. Finally, his declaration prevailed against the combative adversary whom unwillingly moved aside. Slowly the groom and his groomsmen danced and sang their way forward to the front of the room. He stood before the bride's parents who were seated on a throne like bench. Stating his case, his desire to marry the bride, their daughter, he then reiterated his love through songs and dancing. As he makes his plea, music echoed his desire for the bride. Facing the bride's parents, lined up in a handsome row with his groomsmen, together in perfect synchronization they bow and laid prostrate before the parents of the bride. Songs continued echoing his love, asking for the hand of the bride. More proclamations and song were made, begging for the bride to be given to the groom. After a long moment, they stood back up and the groomsmen take a slow step back. Now the groom, standing alone, dressed in a robe of white moves forward and laid prostrate before the bride's parents to beg again for the hand of his bride.

More songs and shouts of proclamation proclaim his desire and love for her. Finally, the parents bless the groom with prayers of affirmation sung over him. The groom has received permission to marry the bride! Prayers, songs of praise, and the gospel is heard!

Almost to the end of this ceremony, the bride enters with her bridesmaids. Jubilant shouts of joy, songs of celebration, rings of dancing swirl the bridal party forward as they progressed toward the groom and her parents. There she meets her beloved husband to be and together they bow, heads down in regal reverence on bended knee, hearts open to the blessing from her parents. The family tree has been extended, the olive branch celebrated, a new member has been confirmed, welcomed and blessed!

The celebration continues with songs of joy and jubilant dancing!

Jesus the bridegroom has entered the village where you reside. But his opponent meets him there. Stones of lies are stacked, towering counterfeit walls cemented, barbwire of deceit rib the gate, and landmines of despair are laid to wage war against Jesus entering to receive you. The adversary fights to block you from knowing Jesus's undeniable love for you. Yet, the one who laid the foundation of the earth, the one who created you, knitted you together, and gave you the very breathe of life is here to redeem you. No battle will prevail against him. Though it may be long, difficult, and ugly. He is a faithful. An undeterred servant, mighty and patient for your redemption story to be birthed, your place at his banquet table is held by his blood grafting you to the tree of life. No adversary can claim victory against him. The end of the battle has been declared. You are chosen! He has fought for you! He has won the battle! A battle fought for the chosen one, the one he loves, the one he has called and given a place in his family.

Tearing down the cemented lies, he rebuilds the foundation of the wall with stones of truth, the barded wired disintegrates by his breath, and the landmines become sinkholes filled with his Living Water. The ground is firm, his foot steady, the battle can only be but a bruise to his heal. His blood has a declaration of victory sprinkled along the path as he enters the village to claim his beloved bride.

Through the battle his eyes were fixed on you, the one he loves so.

He fought for you! The cross was the battle ground against the adversarial enemy, yet Christ has wrought your hand to his. Let the celebration begin! The invitation has been declared. Your acceptance will be moved into the kingdom of God.

The Ketubah
The Wedding Contract or Engagement

The Jewish wedding covenant is called the Ketubah. The Ketubah is a legal contract that spells out the way the husband will provide for his wife and detailing their obligations to one another. This covers circumstances during their marriage, with the occurrence of death, or if there is a reason for a divorce. There is no need for the bride to sign this. This is the intent of the groom, his care and faithfulness to her, his duties, along with the other expectations within their marriage. This may also include her obligation of care for the groom, the household, and their children. Today, more modern ways may have changed this to include the signature of the bride.

The Ketubah resembles the covenants that were made in the Old Testament from God to man. It is important to understand how both are connected to the wedding ceremony. The Ketubah may be written in Aramaic or Hebrew, in calligraphy, and given to the bride for her to keep. In many cases, it becomes a decorative piece that is framed and hung in the home.

The Ketubah demonstrates the great compassion in the Jewish faith. To write a contract listing the requirements of the groom at the time of engagement shows compassion and commitment beyond anything we would see today. Today there are prenuptial agreements that are written to protect the individual's assets instead of providing care for the bride.

A covenant is an agreement between God and His people in which God makes a certain promise. This is the highest level of a covenant. Some covenants require an action or behavior in return. Some synonyms of covenant are: *bond*, *to bind*, *a promise*, *a pact*, and *an agreement*. Covenants are often made between two people.

The engagement time can be short or often too long. In the ancient Jewish culture, it is considered a time to be set apart for one another and legally binding.

This tradition demonstrates how the proposal and engagement are tied together echoing the gospel, we too are set apart and bound to Christ. The elements of the wedding differ through each culture, but there are similarities to be found. Overall, the obvious underlaying thread echoes Jesus Christ's call to us, to be his alone!

Mary and Joseph

> *Because Joseph her husband was faithful to the law, and yet did not want to expose her to public disgrace, he had in mind to divorce her quietly.*
> *(Matthew 1:19)*

Have you ever wondered how Joseph was going to divorce Mary during their engagement, before they were married? The Ketubah should explain this confusion. They were married but had not performed the Nissuin (2nd part). Joseph wanted to quietly divorce Mary to avoid exposing her to public disgrace or worse. I believe this speaks highly of Joseph's character. He was a righteous man with his reputation at stake, but he cared very much about Mary. Yet he knew he was not the father of her child because he had not any physical relations with her. The angel appeared to him and told him not to divorce Mary. He told Joseph Mary had received the Holy Spirit and this child would save the people from their sins. Joseph obeyed; however, his faith was tested. I find it interesting that the man who raised Jesus as his son put aside the law by listening to and obeying God. There were no promises made to Joseph for taking this risk, only a promise of Jesus saving His people from sin.

The Blessing After Accepting Christ's Invitation

> *Behold, I stand at the door and knock, if anyone hears my voice and opens the door, I will come into him and eat with him, and he with me.*
> *(Revelation 3:20)*

After we receive the invitation, either to marriage or to Christ, we are blessed in many ways. In the passage above, it says that Christ will dine with us. When a bride and groom say their vows to one another, they promise, "for better, for worse, in sickness and in health, and for richer or for poorer." Seasons of sorrow and joy will come to a marriage. As you face times of difficulty or blessings, it is good to have someone at your side. Whether you are single or married, you can always have the presence of God with you. When we have a vibrant relationship with Christ through tenacious faithful pursuit of his presence, we will still have times of suffering. With Christ in our life we can be confident in the fact that we will not be suffering alone. He is with us, never leaves us, never stops loving us.

> *You are the God who performs miracles, you display your power among the peoples.*
> *(Psalm 77:14)*

Making a commitment to God will be the best and most powerful earthly and eternal decision one can make. Wouldn't you want to be part of the family of the One who performs miracles? Wouldn't you want to be with the Father who is the very being and essence of love? Are you tired of being hurt and desire to be with the One who will never hurt you, but will bless you and love you unconditionally?

Daily Benefits of Having Christ in Our Life

The best thing about beginning a new day is that we can start over from
yesterday. What a merciful generous gesture God gave us when He created
day and night. New blessings are to come. Every day, God has plans to
fill us with His Fatherly benefits. They include His care, protection, love,
blessings, wisdom and presence.

> *Blessed be the Lord who daily loadeth us with benefits, even*
> *the God of our salvation.*
> *(Psalm 68:19) Selah*

Our only task is to seek, see and receive! Enjoy, call them out in gratitude,
then share. A gift is always multiplied when shared!

> *"Bring the whole tithe into the storehouse, that there may be*
> *food in my house. Test me in this," says the Lord Almighty,*
> *"and see if I will not throw open the floodgates of heaven*
> *and pour out so much blessing that there will not be room*
> *enough to store it."*
> *(Malachi 3:10)*

Have you asked the Lord to fill you today with His benefits? Is there
anything specific you need? What benefits of belonging to Christ do you
notice regularly?

> *"Then the King will say to those on his right, 'Come, you who*
> *are blessed by my Father; take your inheritance, the kingdom*
> *prepared for you since creation of the world."*
> *(Matthew 25:34)*

Think about this. A King whose family you now belong is planning
a feast for you to dine at His table. He is building you a home,
delivering you gifts, and promising eternal benefits to you. Amazing
and irresistible! We get to receive the kingdom of God. This is a benefit
that can never be repaid. All it asks for is a response to this invitation
with belief in Jesus.

He Delights in You

The Lord your God is with you, the Mighty Warrior who saves. He will take great delight in you; in his love he will no longer rebuke you, but will rejoice over you with singing. (Zephaniah 3:17)

So that Christ may dwell in your hearts through faith. And I pray that you, being rooted and established in love, may have power, together with all the Lord's holy people, to grasp how wide and long and high and deep is the love of Christ, and to know this love that surpasses knowledge—that you may be filled to the measure of all the fullness of God. (Ephesians 3:17-19)

Grasping the idea that the Lord your God delights in you may be difficult, though he does. You cannot change facts. We have not yet grasped the fullness of it. Only when we meet him face to face, but he gives us a good measure of his constant tenacious love. And there is always more for us to receive. We can look at the cross and see his suffering for the redemption of our souls, but we may be burdened with our guilt to fully accept and comprehend the meaning behind this act of love. God's love is unconditional, unmitigated, and limitless! It is a yearning love intended to delight. Does this sound crazy? Does it sound wonderful? It is!

Dwell on this Scripture. Read it over and over. Read it as something you know to be true. Grasp it. I encourage you to write a note asking God to open your eyes, ears, and heart so they will see and know his love.

"God loves each of us as if there were only one of us." St. Augustine*

Remember the first element of the wedding? The invitation extended to start the relationship? Jesus invites and calls you, "Come follow me". You are invited into a relationship with him. He is alive! Though you cannot see him, he sees you and is not going to stop pursuing you until the end. His Eursi, the proposal inviting you into an intimate eternal relationship began with his open hands nailed to the cross. He set the price, the Mohar, by the shedding his life blood on the cross. His payment, the blood covenant, was his cup of joy. He drank from the cup and has extended it to you. 'Do this in remembrance of me'. The covenant has been written for you, as your own, the Ketubah.

Special invitations usually require a response or an R.S.V.P. What is your response to Christ's invitation to follow him?

Chapter 2 Questions

1. Do you see the engagement time relating to our waiting time between now and when we meet Jesus face to face? Can you explain this?

2 Do you see any relationship between the marriage contract and your relationship with God?

3. Do you believe that Jesus is a conqueror? That through his death on the cross he died for you?

3

The Brides Preparation

The Mikveh, a Ritual Bath

The Jewish faith celebrates many wedding traditions. The preparation day before the wedding often includes the tradition of the Mikveh bath. The Mikveh bath reflects the Jewish holy day Yom Kippur, or Day of Atonement. This tradition is a look back to the time before the fall in the book of Genesis when Adam and Eve were without sin. It is a cleansing bath intended to reflect the time of purity when man and woman were in the garden before the fall. This ritual is one the bride and groom partake in separately, usually the day before the wedding ceremony. Having been made clean, they will be ready to enter the wedding covenant pure and without sin.

The day before the wedding, the bride and groom partake in ritual cleansing by taking separate Mikvehs. During the bath, they recite prayers, followed by a fast until the wedding day. This ritual is very similar to the holy day of Yom Kippur.

The bride must prepare for the Mikveh. The bath is very much like a baptismal font used in the Christian Church, but it is private. The bride prepares in seclusion. She washes her body and her hair, clips her nails, and has an unusually good scrub down. Once she is ready to enter the Mikveh bath, an attendant will guide her through the ceremonial process. She will recite a prayer as she dips into the water. This is symbolic of the cleansing of sins bringing her back to the state of purity, just as Eve was before the fall.

The blessings or prayer recited in the Mikveh is, "Praise you, Adonai, God of all creation, who sanctifies us with the commandments and commanded us coverings of immersion."

The bride will speak this prayer three times as she rises out of the water. There can also be other blessings said that are tailored to the bride and groom, such as, "Blessed are you, Adonai, ruler of the universe who kept us alive and preserved us and enables us to reach this season."

Think about the picture this ceremony presents. The bride and groom repent of their sins before the wedding ceremony. Consider the significance of the bride and groom entering the wedding covenant cleansed. This is a picture of having their sins taken away. This is beautiful! What rich traditions lay in this faith. All the sins, misdeeds, and mishaps of the past, gone and forgotten. Their slate is wiped clean. They enter a new covenant and become husband and wife, cleansed of sins from the past.

The wedding day is a time when their lives are united, and together they will move forward as one. This is the perfect day. The Jewish faith considers this the day when man and woman symbolically step into the perfect state of the Garden of Eden. So beautiful!

It is easy to see why this day is considered a new beginning. What a perfect way to enter a marriage: with a purified heart before the Lord. You truly are bringing your best to your spouse. You are dressed in a beautiful gown, coiffured hair, seamless makeup, and, most important, a pure heart! Can you imagine the eyes of God as he looks down upon the bride and groom? What blessings would be bestowed upon the bride and groom? All this is considered the happiest and holiest day of life together.

> *Let us rejoice and be glad and give him glory! For the wedding*
> *of the Lamb has come, and his bride has made herself ready.*
> *(Revelation 19:7)*

As believers in Christ, we see that this tradition echoes the mission of Christ for his church, his family. We must ready ourselves to be cleansed before we are presented to Christ. We do this through confession of our sins and by believing in Christ's death and resurrection for our sins. Last of all, Christ asks us to be baptized.

> *Whoever believes and is baptized will be saved, but whoever does not believe will be condemned.*
> *(Mark 16:16)*

> *Dear friends, now we are children of God, and what we will be has not yet been made known. But we know that when Christ appears, we shall be like him, for we shall see him as he is. All who have this hope in him purify themselves, just as he is pure.*
> *(1 John 3:2-3)*

Though we believe in forgiveness through the blood of Christ at the cross exclusively, in the tradition of the Mikveh bath, we can see God's message of salvation. The people of the Old Testament received temporary forgiveness through the sacrifice of animals. This was intended to foreshadow what Christ did for us on the cross, the final sacrifice and permanent payment for all sins.

Learning about the Mikveh bath was one of my first realizations that these wedding traditions reveal the gospel. God is in the details. As we continue to look at the Jewish faith, we will see a beautiful comparison to the church, the body of believers, preparing itself for the day it meets Christ, as well as specific symbols found in the bride's preparation for her wedding day. I hope that you will see both beauty and a depth of faith weaving back and forth throughout this tradition.

Yom Kippur and the Day of Preparation

Within the Old Testament, a description of Yom Kippur is recorded with all its details. Once a year at Passover, the high priest would enter the Tabernacle and move to the farthest point, the Holy of Holies. Here, he would present the blood of a sacrificed animals to cover the entire nation's sins of the last year. However, before he was allowed to enter in to the presence of God, he had to be cleansed. There was a special tunic made for this occasion. What was all the fuss? This was the one time a year that the high priest was allowed to move physically close to God's presence in the Tabernacle. In this moment of intimacy with God, God's presence could be felt, and his Spirit would touch the High Priest. Intimacy with God was the benefit of preparation, but the preparation had to be followed exactly as written. Otherwise, the high priest would literally fall dead. In fact, one necessary procedure before he entered the Holy of Holies was to tie a rope to his foot. That way, if he did not prepare properly and was struck down, another priest would pull him out with the rope.

God is holy; we are not. So, the high priest had to be cleansed and covered to be in God's presence. Today, only when we are covered by the blood of Jesus can we become presentable to stand before God.

> *My guilt has overwhelmed me like a burden too heavy to bear. My wounds fester and are loathsome because of my sinful folly. I am bowed down and brought very low; all day long, I go about mourning.*
> *(Psalm 38:4–6)*

We too must be clean by the blood of Christ before we enter into heaven. Jesus was the perfect unblemished sacrifice. He was sinless, thus covering all sins for all men. Every sin was wiped away at the cross by way of his blood. The work is completed; no more sacrifices are needed.

One of my favorite sayings is, "Repentance is a privilege." I say this because we are fully in God's presence when we repent. There is nothing between us blurring our relationship. Repentance is like cleaning the window that separates us from a beautiful view. Sin smudges our view of God. Repentance removes the grime so we can grasp God's holiness. The problem with the word repentance is that it has a very negative connotation to some people. Maybe it comes from preachers yelling, "Repent and be saved." Instead of sounding like a plea or invitation, it stings like judgement. Laid on top of that is a misunderstanding of why God wants us to repent. Many don't understand the essence of the holiness of God.

The Jewish Faith: Preparing for the Passover

The ancient Jewish faith has a time leading up to the Passover that is set up with steps of preparation. In every household, all the leaven is removed. Leaven is like yeast used to activate dough to rise. In some cultures, leaven symbolizes evil and that which is false. As we study how the bride and groom prepare themselves for their wedding day, remember it is also our story of how we prepare to meet Christ. We want to be ready and prepared. Yes, the planning and participation of the wedding is exciting, but it will pale in comparison to when we meet Christ face-to-face as his bride. Our time with Christ, during repentance, is when we can experience his presence through preparation. As we take time to look into the chambers of our heart and seek the areas of sin we have hidden. He wipes away our sins as we name them, recognize attitudes, words and deeds that have consumed us as we live life without considering his perfect ways. His holiness reflects the way we separated and lived our lives without him. It is my great desire that this study will draw you to the day of preparation, a time of repentance and into his Holy Presence.

During the Mikveh, the bride and groom prepare their hearts as they repent with Yom Kippur prayers. We prepare ourselves through the confession of sins. Listen to Jesus's words:

> *In the same way, I tell you, there is rejoicing in the presence*
> *of the angels of God over one sinner who repents.*
> *(Luke 15:10)*

Did you know that you can make angels sing? If repentance makes angels sing, you know it is pleasing to Jesus. After all, he made the way for us to be forgiven. Look at this scripture and see the next blessing.

> *Peter replied, "Repent and be baptized, every one of you, in*
> *the name of Jesus Christ for the forgiveness of your sins. And*
> *you will receive the gift of the Holy Spirit."*
> *(Acts 2:38)*

Notice the use of the word *gift*. As Jesus was ready to leave this earth, his family, friends, and followers probably had a mixture of emotions; they were sad, scared, and bewildered. The Holy Spirit is part of the Trinity: God the Father, Jesus Christ the Son, and the Holy Spirit. Since the physical departure of Christ, God's presence on earth is manifest as the Holy Spirit. This is a wonderful gift. He is the presence of God that guides us. It is his breath. He leans into us and is our helper. He is gentle and kind, wise and good, yet powerful. He will help us understand the Bible as we study it. He will guide us during our decisions of how to live and will show us where God wants us to be. He can be felt in a powerful way at times. He will strengthen us in tough times. He is comfort in times of sorrow. He will pour joy into our hearts. He will come upon us as we are seeking God, wanting to know him more, and it will make his presence known. He convicts us of our sin. He goes before God when we are praying and will give words to our prayers when we can't find the right ones to express our sorrows and needs. Last of all, he is deposited in our hearts as the promise of salvation. The Holy Spirit testifies to our spirit giving us confidence that we are saved and set aside for Christ for all eternity.

> *"I am going to send you what my Father has promised; but stay in the city until you have been clothed with power from on high."*
> *(Luke 24:49)*

Can you imagine being clothed in the power from on high? Think about what God can accomplish through you now! Your education, lineage, position, and where you live do not matter. God is going to deposit something very powerful in you, and you will be working for his kingdom. This is a very important point. As a believer for over twenty years, the one thing I have observed is that often Christians place God in too small a box. Because we are powerless as humans, we seem to miscalculate how powerful God is amid us. At times we forget that he has given us this authority and power to accomplish his will in our lives.

These are Jesus's last words to us before he left earth:

> Then Jesus came to them and said, "All authority in heaven and on earth has been given to me. Therefore go and make disciples of all nations, baptizing them in the name of the Father and of the Son and of the Holy Spirit, and teaching them to obey everything I have commanded you. And surely I am with you always, to the very end of the age."
> (Matthew 28:18-20)

Make no mistake: Jesus has power and authority over the entire world. Though the Evil One still has power to mess with creation, he does not have authority. There is power in the name of Jesus, as well as authority. Remember this as you speak his name. Repentance leads to some powerful results. Angels sing, and the Holy Spirit will bring power on high to you. As I have said, repentance is a privilege. You end up in God's presence, and he breaks it all out for you. Why not get on your knees start this Mikveh by confessing your sins!

Who Are You Going to Serve?

When I first came to faith, I grasped and absorbed everything I could get my hands on to listen to or read. I had a lot of catching up to do because I was in my thirties. One of the phrases I heard someone say was, "Who is on the throne of your heart?" I believe it may be a tag phrase. It has helped me become aware of idols and my focus on Christ as king.

I have foot issues. A few years ago, I went to the pharmacy to get gel soles for my feet. My friend Lisa suggested I drive across town to a pharmacy that had a machine that could give a more custom fit to my aching feet. I entered the store and headed to the pharmacy. I noticed a young, homeless man close by. Actually, everyone in the store noticed this young man. He was shouting very loudly, "David, it is better to serve in hell than to serve in heaven. David, it is better to serve in hell than to serve in heaven."

I assumed his name was David as he kept repeating this phrase over and over as he paced the aisles. The management of the store could not get him to stop. Eventually, the police were called, and David was escorted out of the store.

The line was drawn very clearly in the sand that day, giving me clarity. I had no idea that Satan was so brazenly after us to serve him. Maybe I did know this, but I hadn't heard it put so clearly. Who are you going to serve? God created us to serve him. The other choice does not come from one who loves you. Who is on the throne of your heart?

An Ezekiel Heart

> *I will sprinkle clean water on you, and you will be clean; I will cleanse you from all your impurities and from all your idols. I will give you a new heart and put a new spirit in you: I will remove from you your heart of stone and give you a heart of flesh. And I will put my spirit in you and move you to follow my decrees and be careful to keep my laws.*
> *(Ezekiel 36:25-27)*

The cleansing of the heart is an inward cleansing. The purpose of the cross was an exchange. As a holy God, he took on our sin and we received his cleansing. Remember the verse in Luke 15 that describes angels rejoicing when one repents? Have you taken the time lately to confess your sins? Don't delay. Allow Christ to sprinkle his living water on you and replace your hard, mechanical heart with a vibrant heart of flesh. Again, repentance is a privilege, but not for the privileged, it is for all mankind. You are coming into God's presence and drawing very close to him as he sits on his throne.

> *All of us have become like one who is unclean, and all our righteous acts are like filthy rags; we all shrivel up like a leaf, and like the wind our sins sweep us away.*
> *(Isaiah 64:6)*

*As for you, you were dead in your transgressions and sins,
in which you used to live when you followed the ways of his
world and of the ruler of the kingdom of the air, the spirit is
now at work in those who are disobedient.
(Ephesians 2:1–2)*

A few years after becoming a Christ follower, I challenged myself to spend over twenty-four hours reflecting on my life, recalling sins, and asking for forgiveness. I was surprised how many hidden sins there were from years past that I had not remembered. As I recalled each sin, I stayed diligent and focused, and repeatedly asked for forgiveness by the blood of Christ. At the end, I imagine a choir of angels were singing. Later in the day, I had a vision that described the picture shown in Ezekiel 36. First, I saw myself dead and lying on a heap of garbage. Then Jesus picked me up and cleansed me. He wiped me with a sponge as he held me, setting me on his knee. As he started to cleanse me, I came to life. I looked up at his face as he wiped down my arms, legs, face, and body. He smiled down with the gentlest smile. Then he reached his hand into my chest and pulled out my heart. It was puny, black, hard, and chiseled. It looked like a piece of charcoal or a black lava rock. He took the sponge and wiped my heart clean. As he did this, my heart transformed. It grew enormous, rosy, and so beautiful. When he finished, I looked up at him, and I said, "It won't fit. It is too big." He looked down at me and smiled and placed my heart back inside me.

What's that in Your Bag?

Years ago, I was going through security at the LAX Airport. On the previous day, I had helped arrange flowers for the wedding of a friend's daughter. I grabbed the same bag I took to the reception to help with the flowers and threw a few things into it as my carry-on bag for my trip.

Security stopped me and asked if I had anything dangerous in my bag. I laughed and said, "No!" The security officer proceeded to pull out a pair of small rose clippers. I had not realized I was carrying them. Then he asked if there was anything else in my bag. I shook my head, hoping there wasn't. He pulled out a pair of large scissors. I was waiting for them to haul me away in handcuffs.

Next, my Bible was pulled from the bag. Holding it in his hand with his pointer finger, he double tapped the Bible, looked me straight in the eye, and said, "Now that, ma'am, is a good book." I flashed him an enormous smile and told him to have a wonderful day. My point is this: you never know what you have packed in that heart of yours that will hide and lie to you. We should carefully look deep into our lives and see where we have made false idols, had bad intentions, given in to anger, and carried those things that do not bring us a righteous life.

A Time of Repentance

Recall your sin. There is no need to work it over mentally. Keep it simple. Ask God to cleanse you from all physical, mental, and emotional bondage by the power of the blood on the cross. Once you get started on this, you will find a rhythm, and this will keep you moving along. Let this flow from your heart. Do not block your emotions. You will get through this, and it will bless you.

If you are engaged or married, ask your fiancé or spouse to do the same. Let this be your own spiritual Mikveh bath. God is cleansing you. He is making you new! He is giving you a new heart.

Let the angels sing! Belt it out! Repentance is a privilege!

Even the Dog Needs Washing

This following story is simple. It is so simple that it could be used for a children's sermon to explain that God is holy, we are not, and why we must be washed before we enter heaven. My friend told me this years ago, and

I think it is a wonderful illustration. If you are an animal lover, hopefully, you will enjoy this.

> I have a dog named Blue who likes to escape from our yard and take field trips up the hill to where the cows live. While my dog is scampering around, his favorite pastime is to roll in the cow pies. This must come from some instinct to cover up his smell. Later, I find my dog sitting on the porch, waiting eagerly to enter the house, hoping to rest up from the excitement of his escapades. Of course, the smell of the cow pies does not go over well with me. He thinks he smells great and is unaware of his filthy condition. Before I can let Blue into the house, I must wash him down with the hose and some soap. This takes some time. By now the cow manure has hardened, and the smell is overwhelming. Once he is clean, he is welcomed into my home. He is given full access to lay where he wants and to languish at my side, under the meal table, or at the end of my bed.

Chapter 3

1. What aspect of the Jewish wedding tradition have you enjoyed so far?

2. Have your views on repentance changed? Do you consider it a privilege to search your heart honestly before God? Or does it challenge you?

3. What steps have you taken to search your heart for hidden and unhidden sins?

4. Have you heard from God while reading this book? Is there something he is whispering to you?

4

The Brides Aroma and Prayer

The Forgiven Woman Anoints Jesus

Luke 7:36–50

The gospels tell the story of a woman anointing Jesus. As we read this, we see she did this as an overflow of her heart. We can assume that she knew she was anointing the feet of her Savior and her King.

> *A woman in that town who lived a sinful life learned that Jesus was eating at the Pharisee's house, so she came there with an alabaster jar of perfume. As she stood behind him at his feet weeping, she began to wet his feet with her tears. Then she wiped them with her hair, kissed them and poured perfume on them. (Luke 7:37-38)*

Another ancient Jewish tradition is that young women would be given a jar of expensive perfume to put in her dowry. This perfume would be costly, about a year's wages. The bride was to use this precious oil to anoint her husband's feet on their wedding night, as well as for household use.

Jesus encounters a worshipper. The sinful woman poured perfume out on Jesus's feet, demonstrating her love for him. This is an unforgettable moment. She demonstrated her love for God with a sweet aroma.

The Pharisee did not offer Jesus the expected hospitality a guest was to receive. He did not wash his feet, give oil for his head, or greet him with a kiss. But this woman who was overwhelmed with the gift of forgiveness and unconditional love by Jesus, gave her most precious gift: her jar of anointing oil and her heart. The jar was broken open so all of it spilled out over his feet. Wiping them with her hair, her tears washed his feet. Have you ever been caught out, so touched by the love of God that you are moved by tears because He has touched your heart so tenderly?

This is a very intimate moment. The sinful woman knew she was a forgiven sinner. Her tears fell, and the aroma of repentance gave her a standing in the writing of the gospel. She demonstrated the receiving of the gift and privilege of being forgiven. As a great sinner, she gave thanks openly because she had experienced the lavish love of forgiveness. Her heart was moved and open. The sinful woman's heart was healed of its darkness. Then Jesus said, "Your faith has saved you; go in peace."

A Sweet Aroma and Tears

What can we do to return this great love? Prayer is the essence of our relationship with God. If you are now in a relationship with him, He wants to talk with you. Tell him your problems, ask for help, say thank you for all your gifts, sing to him, confess to him, and tell him you love him.

No one had to tell the sinful woman how to worship Jesus. It overflowed from her heart. The deep recognition of her sins and his love brought deep worship, an overflowing, an exultation from her heart. No one needs to tell you to worship Jesus if you spend time in His presence it will just happen. You won't be able to resist. Prayer, praise, sacrificial love, and obedience will spill forth from your heart as you draw close to him and catch the aroma of his sacrifice on the cross.

Be moved, stirred, and open to the aroma of his sweet presence.

The aroma of love is something we all want. Beautiful bottles of perfume are designed to pull at our hearts and our wallets.

This woman, with her tears, stopped a dinner party attended by some very prominent people. As tears fell, the silence was heard between her sobs.

This may have made the guests at the dinner party a bit uncomfortable, but Jesus did not ask her to stop. This was a moment of worship, a very public display. The dinner guests were uncomfortable with her worship, and people will be with yours!

Tears are a part of life. Tears pour forth when a heart is stirred, moved, and opened. Often when a person gives his or her life to Christ, there are tears as God removes the hardness of the heart with the beautiful gentleness of his grace. The heart softens as we experience freedom from our sins. Do you want to be moved with sweet tears of love? The tears of forgiveness can be yours, and the aroma of thanksgiving can be released as you accept Jesus and allow him to wash over you with his cleansing blood.

Here is a poem I wrote about the forgiven woman.

Cracked Open

Drawing close, heart spills the rot of my soul.
The presence of his aroma washes over,
Cracked open, sins on the floor,
Forgiveness covers my rot.
Falling to his feet, presence sweet,
Hair searching for his crown,
Overcome.
Moved, stirred, tears spilled,
Sins revealed fall.
Forgiven sinner tastes lavish love.
The sweet aroma of forgiveness covers,
Rot gone, caught on a cross.
Moved to sin no more,
Stirred by his presence.
His sweet aroma has become my own!
Lavish Love!

Imagine the forgiven woman at the end of the evening after she had returned home. Her hair is still covered with the perfumed oil she poured on Jesus's feet. As she lays in bed, the lingering aroma fills her room. The perfume is contained within the walls, but her heart knows no bounds. Does she smell the perfume, or does she smell worship and forgiveness? Tears roll down her face as she remembers the moment she was forgiven. She remembers the moment at the feet of her Savior. Did the words he spoke echo as she looked up into the night?

"Your sins are forgiven. Your sins are forgiven. Your faith has saved you. Your faith has saved you. Go in peace. Go in peace."

I can't help but imagine that the forgiven woman did not wash her hair for a very long time. She may have savored the sweet smell of perfume, the aroma of worship, and the aroma of intimacy with her Savior. Have you recognized how your sin smelled and was covering your heart with rot before the forgiveness of your Savior? Smell His sweet aroma!

Privileged Territory

Not only is the bride beautiful to look at, she is beautiful to smell! While congratulating the bride and groom during the wedding reception, you may catch the sweet smell of her preparations. Then you will know you are in privileged territory! Certainly, others benefit from her preparations, but there is one person to whom she wants to smell perfect: her beloved groom. To him, she will be more than a pleasing aroma!

The Bride's Preparation

> You love righteousness and hate wickedness; therefore God, your God, has set you above your companions by anointing you with the oil of joy. All your robes are fragrant with myrrh and aloes and cassia; from palaces adorned with ivory the music of the strings makes you glad.
> (Psalm 45:7-8)

The bride's aroma is an important and beautiful part of her wedding day. From early in the day, fragrances are layered upon her. First, she is lathered with the finest soap, shampoo, body oils, lotions, hair spray, and perfume. The perfume could be an old familiar favorite or something new for this special day. The very last layer of scent will come from her bouquet of flowers, a handful of aromas she will carry into the wedding ceremony.

What is your favorite scent?

Certainly, flowers bear symbolism and significance while also producing a variety of aroma and beauty. For instance, the rose symbolizes love and passion, while also being known for its fragrance. Orange blossoms represent fertility. The gardenia symbolizes joy, and the hydrangea symbolizes perseverance. Every bride has flowers she loves, depending on color, scent, and some sort of sentimental significance. The wedding is her time to have her bouquet just as she wants it.

> *But thanks be to God, who always leads us as captives in Christ's triumphal procession and uses us to spread the aroma of the knowledge of him everywhere. For we are to God the pleasing aroma of Christ among those who are being saved and those who are perishing. To the one we are an aroma that brings death; to the other, an aroma that brings life. And who is equal to such a task?*
> *(2 Corinthians 2:14-16)*

Our Fragrance

> *May my prayer be set before you like incense; may the lifting of my hands be like the evening sacrifice.*
> *(Psalm 141:2)*

Consider how we can cover ourselves with a sweet smell as we approach the presence of God. Prayers are like a sweet fragrance to God. There is an abundance of scripture comparing prayer to aroma, incense, and fragrance. Since all of man is created uniquely in the image of God, our prayers, the release of our individual sweet fragrance, is what we produce as we pause before the throne of God and converse with him.

Prayer is communication with God. We know that there are many types of communication. Of course, there is speech, the written word, and music. Technology provides us with blogging, Instagram, Twitter, and other forms of electronic communication. They all convey a thought to another human being. Conversations can be short or drawn out. Words convey emotions of joy, sadness, laughter, instruction, love, tenderness, anger, and more. All these emotions are acceptable to use while praying. So, when you think about praying to God, break out of any stereotype and recognize that you were created individually and will have your own way of talking with God. God knows you and sees you. He already knows what you feel and what you need. Talk to him and make it real. He created language so that we would talk to him.

There are certain scriptures that talk about how prayer is like an incense that lifts to God. I picture a Native American laying blankets over an open fire to send smoke signals up; all the while he is chanting prayers. However, prayers do not dissipate as smoke does. They land in God's ears, and he hears them as they part from your lips and land in a bowl made from gold.

> *The eyes of Lord are on the righteous and his ears are attentive*
> *to their cry.*
> *(Psalm 34:15a)*

I have a picture in my head, though not from scripture. God is creating a beautiful masterpiece with all the prayers of mankind. Like the Wailing Wall, I see a long wall with little strips of our prayers from every nation and age of humanity. The prayers have turned into gold, silver, stones of ruby, jasper, topaz, emeralds, jade, and pearl. These prayers create a beautiful tapestry. Maybe someday, we will see how God lifted our needs, placing it as an answered prayer, and turned into a beautiful memorial. Maybe we will be able to walk up and stand in front of it, and hear the prayer requests parting from our lips, from all our brothers and sisters in Christ, from every native tongue, and hear God's answer! Can you imagine how incredible it would be?

Another angel, who had a golden censer, came and stood at
the altar. He was given much incense to offer, with the prayers
of all God's people, on the golden altar in front of the throne.
(Revelation 8:3)

Can you see how prayers are so important, God puts them on a golden
altar, in a golden bowl? Our words are not meaningless to him. Why would
he want something he did not value to be contained in a golden bowl? In
fact, in the original Tabernacle, the laver of incense was the tallest piece
of furniture. This demonstrates that our highest calling is praying to
God. Our words are precious to him. Prayer is what connects us to God.
When prayers are answered, we start to get a glimpse of his majesty and
compassion. Answered prayer demonstrates his power, mercy, and love.
Prayer is how we get to know God. It is how we see who he is. Once you
start to see how God can answer prayer, you will be awed, and your faith
in God as the power on high will be certifiably secure.

When I first became a believer, a follower of Christ, a friend invited
me to a retreat. The presenter of the retreat, Liz Curtis Higgins, was
very funny. During one speech, she was on a roll. She had us in a
constant state of laughter. As I scanned the room, a very pretty woman
caught my eye. What I noticed about her was that she looked sad while
everyone was laughing. I said a simple prayer. It went something like
this: "Lord, she looks so sad. Make her happy." After all, this was a
weekend away, and I thought everyone should be enjoying themselves.
Well, I forgot about the prayer. Liz was talking, everyone was quietly
listening, and then, suddenly, the pretty woman across the room was
out of control with laughter. She could not stop herself. Liz stopped
talking, and the whole room was staring at this woman. Her laughter
was so loud that she had to leave the room. It was then that I realized
God was showing me that prayer is powerful and not to ignore this
opportunity. I imagine Liz was feeling pretty good about her story too!

Scripture teaches us a lot about God and prayer. It demonstrates how man calls
out in prayer and records God's response. This is shown throughout the Bible.
King David prayed these following words with such fervor. It is encouraging

to know that a king from the lineage of Christ was desperate as he prayed. On his own, he was powerless, but he knew where his help came from.

> *Listen to my words, Lord, consider my lament.*
> *Hear my cry for help,*
> *my King and my God,*
> *for to you I pray.*
> *In the morning, Lord, you hear my voice;*
> *in the morning I lay my requests before you*
> *and wait expectantly.*
> *(Psalm 5:1-3)*

What prayers have you laid out in expectation to hear from God? Imagine God sitting on the throne, leaning over the side of it, with His head tilted so that He can hear you. He is eager to hear from you. He is waiting to hear your voice, your words of thanks, and your cries for help. He takes in all your prayers. We each have a uniqueness that can only be known by our creator.

Old Testament Sacrifices

> *He is to take a censer full of burning coals from the altar before the Lord and two handfuls of finely ground fragrant incense and take them behind the curtain. He is to put the incense on the fire before the Lord, and the smoke of the incense will conceal the atonement cover above the tablets of the covenant law, so that he will not die.*
> *(Leviticus 16:12-13)*

I won't go into a lot of detail about how sacrifices were made in the Old Testament. But when the priests were preparing the sacrifice, there was a bowl of incense burning at the same time. To put it simply, no matter what good things we do for God, there is always a bit of our selfish desire in it. No matter how secretive we are about something we do for someone, we are still patting ourselves on the back for doing so. Because of this, they could not help but taint their sacrifices of care, generosity, and hard work;

therefore, incense was a necessary symbol to cover their pride. Today, our sin is covered by Christ's sacrifice on the cross.

In the book of Leviticus, it explains how things were done before Jesus became the sacrificial final sacrifice to cover all sins.

Don't worry if all of this doesn't make sense. The point is, in this image, the fire burns the incense to cover the stench of sin. As I said before, no matter how perfectly we try to do the right thing, we are still imperfect before God. It is the rot of our sin that smells. Even the high priest, who follows all the strict instructions of purity, has a stench of sin. Today we are covered with the final sacrifice of Christ, the perfect sacrifice (and fragrance). It is his blood and his gift of grace that cleanses us and allows us to come before him. We no longer smell!

> *Blessed is the one whose transgressions are forgiven, whose sins are covered. Blessed is the one whose sin the Lord does not count against them and in whose spirit is no deceit.*
> *(Psalm 32:1-2)*

The Persistent Widow
Luke 18:1–8

Jesus told this parable to paint a story picture of how we should be persistent about prayer. For those of you who may start your prayers with a phrase like, "Here I am again, Lord," there is no need. He wants us to understand to not give up. He is encouraging us through this illustration of a widow to be relentless in our pursuit of the ask. If ever there is a person who was in a weak societal position, it was a widow. Overall, women were not treated well in this male-dominated culture. This woman was without a spouse, so she had no man to defend her or speak for her. She was being mistreated by someone, and she had no way to free herself from it other than going before a judge. The judge was her only chance, her last chance. And the judge was supposed to be a fair advocate; however, he did not give a hoot about her and spoke openly about how he did not fear God or care about people. Her situation could not be worse. But she had an iron will. She had the tenacity and the blood of a mule.

I believe she was one of the few stalkers in the Bible. She was relentless in demanding that the judge grant justice. Imagine her waiting in the court halls to catch him coming back from lunch so she could ask him once more for justice. Can't you just see her standing behind him in line every time he bought a coffee or a newspaper? She became his shadow. She demanded justice. And she drove him crazy, so finally, he gave her justice just to escape her.

What about you? Are you relentless as you pray? Do you refuse to give up and continue to plead your case to God? That judge was not a fair man. He did not follow the rules laid out for judges in Second Chronicles. This judge should have not been allowed to hold his seat. How much more just is our God? He is a God who cannot tolerate injustice.

If a judge were somehow connected to a case, he would have to excuse himself from it. But not so with our God. He is so entangled with our case. He has a desire to make sure that our requests are heard. But overall, we should be asking what his will is. It is through his will that he will be glorified. When God is glorified, we start to get a glimpse of his character. We see how compassionate and powerful he is. He does not abuse his power to neglect or repress the weak. No, he does quite the opposite. He pursues us because he wants to help us and carry us when we are suffering. He wants us to know the depth of his love.

Christ was glorified at the resurrection. It was his greatest act for all of humanity. So, when you hear that God wants to be glorified, it is not the same glory we desire. It is a glory that displays his splendor through his selfless act for us. It is his glory that displays his power over the evil one for our redemption.

When it comes to the matter of prayer, God is always available. I have been praying the same prayer for many years. I know there are stacks and stacks in the golden bowl of incense. But, God has sustained me through the time as I have waited to see the answer to this prayer. It is not easy to wait for answers. The other day I had my usual conversation with God about this prayer I have persistently pleaded for years. I asked him for evidence that he was at work in this person's life. It was then I noticed this person was crying a lot. Those tears spoke deep to my heart, God is at work. The parable of the Persistent Widow encourages us. But note that the persistent widow knew that the judge had the power to change her life, to take down her adversary, and to restore her peace. My friend, acknowledge who God is and be bold! Be persistent!

Chapter 4 Questions

1. What do you think about the bride and the details of her aroma?

2. What do you think of the comparison of the aroma to your prayers?

3. What symbolism have you enjoyed learning about?

4. Is there anything about your prayer life you want to change?

5. How do you see confession and prayer tying together?

5

The Bride, her Veil, and the Queen

The Story of Queen Esther

The Book of Esther is the story is of a young orphaned Jewish girl and an unlikely choice to be a queen that becomes the heroine of her nation. Esther and her Uncle Mordecai's obedience to God, allowed Esther to advance from orphan to queen. Esther stood before the King Xerxes and requested his presence at dinner, risking her life so that a nation could be saved. Esther knew the Jewish people were people of prayer, and as she approached her time with the king she fasted and prayed. She prepared herself with the sacrifice of fasting to be in communion with God before she approached King Xerxes. She knew her God would hear the prayers of the Jewish people, so she trusted that He would make a way. She had the choice of being used by God to save a nation. So, she prepared herself through the Jewish practice of sacrifice through prayer and fasting.

As a bride, you are considered the queen for the day. As a child of God, you have been adopted into the bloodline of Christ, and you now belong to a king. Yet, we do not need to risk our lives to approach the throne of God. We are his ambassador and are called to step out like Esther. Our lives have been exchanged for Christ's, our old sinful flesh has been given new life, and we are part of a kingdom which may call us to put our lives on the line, just as Esther did.

In the ancient Jewish wedding tradition of the Mikveh bath, the bride will fast. As followers of Christ, we are called to fast. Jesus said, "Whenever you fast, do not put on a gloomy face as the hypocrites do, for they neglect their appearance so that they will be noticed by men when they are fasting" (Matthew 6:16).

Isn't it interesting Esther fasted three days and Christ was buried for three days before His resurrection? The Old Testament continues to point us to Christ. In Esther 5:1, it says that on the third day, Esther put on the royal robes and stood in the inner court of the palace, in front of the king's hall. The symbolism cannot be missed. As Esther approached the king at the risk of losing her life, she saved a nation. Christ died and was buried for three days, a time in which he neither ate nor drank. He made a way for all of mankind to be saved.

The life of a believer is an unbalanced exchange. We belong to a King, adopted into his bloodline by his sacrifice. We receive eternal life and escape the punishment of our sins. We are given a new heart and the Holy Spirit to guide us and fill us with His holy presence. We have nothing to offer to our creator. Our hands are empty. Esther had neither money nor privilege to offer, but as an orphan, she was given the opportunity to offer her life to God.

We do not know how God is going to use us. We must emulate Esther and obey. Esther knew the stakes were high as she approached the king. She had determined before she started to fast, "If I perish, I perish." Then she fasted and submitted herself to God and His will to save a nation. The story ends as God intended: the Jewish nation was saved. But the beauty of the story is not that she became queen, but that she was willing to exchange her life and lay it down for the will of God. Most of us will not have such a dramatic story. But we are all called like Esther to serve our King Jesus. He has a plan for us. He has called us to be part of the story of calling mankind to respond to his invitation to join the kingdom of God. However mundane or unheroic your calling, it is the beauty and willingness of your obedience which pleases your King. Today, the Jewish nation celebrates the story of Esther with the holy day of Purim. Know this, Christ celebrates your obedience with every little step along the way. Sometimes it is the dying of the flesh in the everyday mundane things but, seem so insignificant are significant to our God.

The Bride

> *Now Joshua was dressed in filthy clothes as he stood before the*
> *angel. The angel said to those who were standing before him.*
> *"Take off his filthy clothes." Then he said to Joshua, "See I have*
> *taken away your sin, and I will put fine garments on you."*
> *(Zechariah 3:3–4)*

To me, there is not a more beautifully dressed woman in the fashion world than the bride. Some magazine pictures have the bride standing in the middle of an expanse of grass as she looks like a budding white flower.

There is a song for the moment a bride walks down the aisle, making all heads turn and wait. As the bride turns the corner and walks down the aisle, we study every detail, from her head to her toe, taking it in as a portrait. We study her coiffured hair, the train of her dress, and the details of her veil. There is an obvious reason she is expected to walk slowly. We want to soak up every detail of her beauty. As Christ followers, we are preparing to wear a new garment to attend the wedding as his beloved guest and his honored bride.

> *I saw the Holy City, the new Jerusalem, coming down out*
> *of heaven from God, prepared as a bride beautifully dressed*
> *for her husband.*
> *(Revelation 21:2)*

The Groom

In the Jewish tradition, the groom may wear a robe called a Kittel. It is a white linen robe that Jewish men wear on high holidays and at their burial. The bride may give this to her husband as a wedding gift. It is a Yom Kippur robe that is traditionally worn as a reminder to "awake him to repent." These days, a groom's attire can be anything from a tuxedo to a pair of shorts.

King and Queen for the Day

In the Jewish tradition, the bride and groom are queen and king on their wedding day. This is very different from Christian or secular weddings today where there seems to be more concern with the happiness of those attending. In the ancient Jewish tradition, the focus is on every wish the bride and groom may have.

Scripturally, we know God sits on the throne of heaven. Alongside him, Christ waits for his bride, the church or family of believers. So, it is fitting this Jewish tradition emulates what the church will look like in heavenly eternity. We will be part of a royal family, adopted through Christ's bloodline. Since Christ is the King, it is fitting for his bride to wear a crown. The apostle Paul explains it best:

> *I have fought the good fight, I have finished the race, I have kept the faith. Now there is in store for me the crown of righteousness, which the Lord, the righteous judge, will award to me on that day—and not only to me, but also to all who have longed for his appearing.*
> *(2 Timothy 4:7-8)*

We will receive our crowns one day, although the passage does not give the exact details of what we must do to receive these many crowns. The author Paul states it simply, "Fight the good fight." That would be staying faithful where God has placed you. Stand strong. Finish the race. We are racing against time to share the gospel in whatever way he has called us to share. It may be living in faithfulness among unbelievers, loving the unlovable, or working in the city to serve God. It could be anything as we are keeping the faith. Maybe it is to pray continually. Maybe it to resist sin in front of those watching you and disparaging you for doing so. Maybe it is the simple act of staying with those who so desperately need the love of God. The bottom line is that God is watching, and he is pleased when you are working for him, his kingdom. You are already saved, but you are saved to do his good work, to fight the good fight to further the gospel. His design from the beginning was to use man to work with him in the fields to bring about the salvation of mankind. The Bible is full of stories of people serving God to do his will. These were not perfect people, but they were those willing to go where God calls them and to work alongside those who did not know God. He will reward you for your faithfulness. It is not easy to be a follower of Christ, but he is going to reward you with crowns—not here on earth, but in heaven. Yes, you will be blessed here, but an even greater reward is being saved up.

> *Therefore put on the full armor of God, so that when the day of evil comes, you may be able to stand your ground, and after you have done everything, to stand. Stand firm then, with the belt of truth buckled around your waist, with the breastplate of righteousness in place, and with your feet fitted with the readiness that comes from the gospel of peace. In addition to all this, take up the shield of faith, with which you can extinguish all the flaming arrows of the evil one. Take the helmet of salvation and the sword of the Spirit, which is the word of God.*
> *(Ephesians 6:13-17)*

This last scripture gives a visual guide for how to follow Paul's plea. These instruments of armor instruct us to dress ourselves with God's tools until we are given that robe of righteousness one day.

This isn't the most glamorous outfit compared to that of the bride, but it is what we will be trading in. When I turn in my armor I want it to be tattered from faithfulness, full of persecution dents, and thread bear from running the race. We will not need the armor of God in heaven. Peace will reign. Joy will not be contained. And the good fight will be celebrated. Your crown and new robe are awaiting you. Stand strong, fight the good fight, and keep the faith.

The Bride's Veil
Rebekah

There is another story in Genesis that demonstrates how a woman set herself aside for her future groom by using a veil. This story of romance picks up as she is about to meet Isaac.

> *And Isaac went out to meditate in the field toward evening. And he lifted his eyes and saw, that behold, there were camels coming. And Rebekah lifted up her eyes, and when she saw Isaac, she dismounted from the camel and said to the servant, 'Who is that man, walking in the field to meet us?" The servant answered, "It is my master." So she took her veil and covered herself. And the servant told Isaac all the things that he had done. Then Isaac brought her into the tent of Sarah his mother and took Rebekah, and she became his wife, and he loved her. So Isaac was comforted after his mother's death. (Genesis 24:63-67)*

Rebekah's intention of placing the veil over her face was to demonstrate to Isaac she agreed to be set aside for him and she was anticipating the moment when he would look upon her face, see her beauty, and share the intimacy of being husband and wife. She was demonstrating she was yearning for this intimacy with her future husband. Rebekah had agreed to marry Isaac before she met him. The placing of the veil over her face as she prepared to meet her future husband was romantic. It meets all the requirements of modesty and, in doing so, it protects and prepares for intimacy.

The Veil

> *Then Moses said, "Now show me your glory." (Exodus 33:18)*

In the ancient Jewish tradition, there is a ceremony in which the groom sees his bride before the wedding. This is called the Bedken. This is the time when she is veiled, sitting on a throne, waiting for the groom, family, and friends to stop by. The groom will come in lift the veil to look upon her face. He may even sing her love songs as he studies her beauty. After a long pause, he will gently lower the veil over her face.

In the Old Testament, a young man by the name of Jacob worked for seven years to marry Rachel, but her father tricked him, and he ended up marrying Rachel's sister, Leah, instead. This trick was accomplished by cloaking the bride behind a veil. The veils during this time were very heavy, not translucent and refined as they are today. The tradition of the Bedken is to lift the veil before the ceremony to confirm that the right woman is behind it.

Can you imagine the intensity of anticipation in the groom as he stands before his bride, looking earnestly upon her face, their eyes searching one another, speaking a thousand words with just a look? The veil is lowered over her face, and he knows the bride is his.

The veil symbolizes modesty, respect, and acts as a protection of intimacy. The only person allowed to lift the veil is the groom, and this privilege of intimacy is his alone. This is a moment that we all love to watch as the groom ever so gently lifts the veil and admires the beauty of his bride.

In Exodus 33, Moses was very eager to know God. Then Moses said, "Please show me your glory." And the Lord said, "I will cause all my goodness to pass in front of you, and I will proclaim my name, the Lord, in your presence. I will have mercy on whom I will have mercy, and I will have compassion on whom I will have compassion. But," he said, "you cannot see my face, for no one may see me and live." Then the Lord said, "There is a place near me where you may stand on a rock. When my glory passes by, I will put you in a cleft in the rock and cover you with my hand until I have passed by. Then I will remove my hand and you will see my back; but my face must not be seen."

The Old Testament has quite a few images concerning the veil. Let us explore the meaning of the veil. The Webster definition of a veil is "a thin or light fabric, worn over the face or head for concealment, protection, or ornamentation." Second, it is "a piece of cloth, like a curtain, which covers and conceals." The symbolism of the veil has great depth as it relates to the elements of the wedding, the Jewish faith, and an intimate relationship with God.

God had said He knew Moses by name, and He found favor with him. This meant He considered Moses a friend. Moses sought more from God. Moses wanted to know God and desired to draw closer to Him as he guided the nation of Israel. God covered Moses with his hand. His hand was used as a veil to hide the glory of God, which we will all see one day. God is reserving his full glory to be revealed to us when we meet up with him. It's great Moses had such desire and confidence in his relationship with God to ask this. Furthermore, God did not deny him this because he was undeserving. We can see how, through the span of the Bible, its message weaves together seamlessly. God is reserving himself for us when we meet. We should be like Moses and seek God earnestly, asking for more.

God allows Moses to be in his presence as he passes by him, hidden by the hand of God. At this time, God proclaims his name.

As he spent time with Moses talking to him, some of it was instruction on how to lead the people of Israel. The result of meeting with God deposited God's glory leaving Moses's face radiant when he returned. Hopefully you have seen the look of radiance on a person who is full of joy. Hopefully, you have experienced this joy at some moment in your life.

> *When Moses finished speaking to them, he put a veil over his face. But whenever he entered the Lord's presence to speak with him, he removed the veil until he came out. And when he came out and told the Israelites what he had been commanded, they saw that his face was radiant. Then Moses would put the veil back over his face until he went in to speak with the Lord.*
> *(Exodus 34:33–35)*

The Tabernacle and the Veil

The temple was designed to have a curtain or some text call it a veil. This stood between the Tent of Meeting and the Tabernacle, where the Ark of the Covenant rested. Behind this veil the presence of God resided. The veil was a barrier and a separator between God and man. Only the high priest could go past the veil and be in God's presence once a year. It was a time of intimacy with God.

In Leviticus 4, the priest was required to sprinkle the blood of the sacrificed bull on the front of the veil of the sanctuary seven times before entering. The veil guards the holiness of God. In Isaiah 59, it states our sins have made a separation between you and your God; they have hidden his face so that he does not hear. The veil guards what is holy. It stands between God and us. The blood of the sacrificed bull sanctified the entering through the veil to be in the presence of God. The blood of Christ sanctifies us, allowing us to enter through him to be in the presence of God.

The Veil in the Temple

> And when Jesus had cried out again in a loud voice, he gave up
> his spirit. At that moment the curtain of the temple was torn
> in two from top to bottom. The earth shook, the rocks split.
> (Matthew 27:50-51)

Jesus was on the cross when he breathed his last breath. At this moment, the veil in the temple tore from bottom to top. As the veil of the temple was torn, the sacrifice on the cross was complete, and now we have a full access to God through Jesus. The old way of doing things is gone. Christ was the last and final sacrifice. A perfect sacrifice. Now man and God are no longer separated. Jesus is here with full access!

God kept his plan and the message of intimacy with man through these details, moving forward through Rebekah, Moses, and Rachel. All of it pointed to the time of Christ on the cross. Christ is here as our mediator between God the Father and us. We no longer need a high priest to perform sacrifices for us. We now have full access to the presence of God, and we can experience this intimacy with God ourselves. This is a new time. Most people in the Old Testament did not have access to this level of intimacy with God. They had representatives who did this for them. We no longer need anyone to speak to God for us. We can be in God's presence. We can talk directly to him and ask him directly to forgive our sins. We can sit with him and enjoy all the benefits of his presence.

The veil has been torn, lifted, and Christ is present.

Chapter 5 Questions

1. What about the veil was significant to you?

2. What is the importance of the bride's gown as it relates to the gospel?

3. Is there a veil over your heart that needs to be lifted to know God?

6

The Place Where It All Happens

The Huppah and the Yichud
The Tent and the Wedding Chamber

> *Now Moses used to take a tent and pitch it outside the camp,*
> *far off from the camp, and he called it the tent of meeting.*
> *And everyone who sought the Lord would go out to the tent*
> *of meeting, which was outside the camp.*
> *(Exodus 33:7)*

The huppah is used during the Jewish wedding ceremony and symbolizes the bride and groom's home. It resembles a canopy or tent modeled after the homes the Israelites used when they lived in the desert. It is square shaped. The sides can open and sometimes the roof as well. The four poles may be carved of wood or decorated. Often, a prayer shawl called a tallit is laid over the top of the huppah to symbolize that this union is covered by prayer. Many times, the tallit is a gift from the bride to the groom.

Unlike American traditions, the bride and groom's families are near one other during the wedding ceremony. They usually stand inside the huppah along with the bride, groom, and rabbi. The spirit of it is two families are being brought together.

The requirements of the huppah are simple. The sides are open, and there is no furniture in it except a small table which holds a cup of wine. This is a reminder, the Jewish home is about people, not possessions. As the groom is waiting for his bride, he fills the huppah with love songs. The groom stands in the huppah before the bride enters. This establishes him as the leader of their home, the provider of their family and a reminder he has invited her into this covenant relationship.

Where does the huppah idea originate? Like most traditions, there is a rich history behind it. The Israelites traveled in the desert in tents for forty years. Additionally, the home of Abraham and Sarah was a tent. Since Abraham is the father of the Jewish faith, many aspects of his daily life, such as his home, are remembered and celebrated.

> *And behold, the word of the Lord came to him: "This man shall not be your heir; your very own son shall be your heir. And he brought him outside and said, "Look toward heaven, and number the stars, if you are able to number them." Then he said to him, "So shall your offspring be."*
> *(Genesis 15:4–5)*

God promised Abraham that he would be the father of a great nation. The promise was fulfilled in Abraham's son, Isaac. Isaac married his wife, Rebekah, in his mother's tent.

This tradition of the huppah can be traced back through the centuries. Under the stars, families are grounded by faith in God's provision and promises.

The huppah resembling the structure of a tent is a reminder to the Jewish people of a time when they lived in a foreign land, waiting for the permanent home that was promised by God. Even the Tabernacle, the place where God resided and which the Israelites carried around in the desert for forty years, was mobile like a tent. Today, we are waiting for the day we are united with God and given a permanent home in his kingdom. At the end of Ephesians 2, it talks about how we are being built together in a dwelling place for God by the Spirit. In Christ, we are no longer residing in tents that blow around, but we are now on a solid ground with Jesus as our cornerstone.

> *By day the Lord went ahead of them in a pillar of cloud to guide them on their way and by night in a pillar of fire to give them light, so that they could travel by day or night. Neither*

the pillar of cloud by day nor the pillar of fire by night left
its place in front of the people.
(Exodus 13:21-22)

The Israelites would follow God's lead and move forward, or they would stay according to how he directed them by a pillar of fire during the night and a cloud during the day.

The ideal place for a Jewish wedding to be held is under the open sky, directly under the creator of the universe, without any veils of separation. The stars carry an immense amount of significance to those of the Jewish faith.

The following is what the huppah symbolizes on the wedding day:

- An open inviting home.
- A focus on people, not possessions.
- Following God's lead as he directs your household.
- Being filled with worship music.
- The husband as the leader of the home and family.

Remember that these are traditional ideals. They are not absolutes in today's home.

As the bride approaches the huppah, the groom will step out to escort her into the tent. Symbolically, he is welcoming her into the home that he has set up for them. The American tradition that parallels this occurs when the groom carries the bride over the threshold of their new home.

When the bride enters the huppah, she will circle her husband seven times. Her mother and mother-in-law may escort her as she does this. Why seven times? There are many different recorded reasons for this, some more ancient, some more modern. Notice that all of them tie back to the history of the Jewish faith. Here are some explanations:

1. God created the earth in seven days.
2. As the bride walks around her husband seven times, she is building a wall of protection around him from the allure of others.

3. Seven is the traditional number of the holy days, and the Sabbath is on the seventh day.
4. The phrase "when man takes a wife" is written in the Torah seven times.
5. When Joshua walked around the city of Jericho seven times, he conquered it. So, the bride walks around her groom to break down the walls of his heart to allow her access.
6. There are seven matriarchs of the faith: Eve, Sarah, Rebekah, Rachel, Tamar, Ruth, and Esther.
7. The number seven is the number of completeness.

> As the bride circles her groom, she is to pray, "Blessed is she who has come. May the Holy One, He who understands the love of a bride, may He bless the groom and the bride."

Under the huppah is where the bride and groom start their covenant marriage. Since the Christian Bible contains a version of the Torah, as well as references to it, Christian believers also recognize the significance of the number seven. One of Jesus's teachings adds yet another level of significance to this number in Matthew 18, when Jesus teaches how many times one must forgive:

> *Then Peter came and said to Him, "Lord, how often shall my brother sin against me and I forgive him? Up to seven times?" Jesus *said to him, "I do not say to you, up to seven times, but up to seventy times seven.*
> *(Matthew 18: 21-22)*

This is good advice to keep a marriage and any other important relationship in your life healthy and happy. Forgiveness helps you to move forward to a new time of healing, and it matures us as individuals and as marriage partners. Forgiveness takes the bitterness of grudges and all other hurts we hold onto and starts to loosen us up so that our breath of life is fuller. Forgiveness has benefits of health and well-being added to the relational benefit. Forgiveness can become a lifestyle. Forgiveness can be beautiful but does not negate our sorrow. It is a mode we can use to move forward in life and heal ourselves and our relationships. God is the Father of forgiveness. As Jesus was on the cross, he said, "Father, forgive them, for they do not know what they are doing." Jesus set the standard. In suffering through the pain of the cross, he did as he taught us. He asked his Father to extend the hand of forgiveness to us.

The Yuchid
A Time of Intimacy for the Bride and Groom.

> *That is why a man leaves his father and mother and is united*
> *to his wife, and they become one flesh.*
> *(Genesis 2:24)*

The consummation of the marriage seals the covenant. The physical laying together as husband and wife, and enjoying the benefit of becoming one flesh, makes marriage legal by many standards and across many cultures and faiths.

Becoming one flesh is part of God's design to physically tether man and woman. This was God's plan: to bring man and woman pleasure so they would become one flesh. The term "to become one flesh" is difficult to define. It is the physical act of intercourse, but it is also the entwining of lives. The boundaries between the two will become blurred as you share your life with one another. You are building a life together, building a relationship together that becomes its own. You go from a "me" adding to yourself a "we." It is the "we" that over the years starts to feel very much like one flesh.

We do not get too far along in the Bible before we see that God's plan was to bless Abraham and fulfill the covenant of Genesis 15. It was through the physical union of a man and woman that he accomplished this plan. In the Jewish faith, a man is considered incomplete until he is married and has children. God's design was to use a man and woman to build the human race. As Abraham is considered the father of their faith, let us look at how he struggled with this privilege of building a family.

After this, the word of the Lord came to Abram in a vision: "Do not be afraid, Abram. I am your shield, your very great reward." But Abram said, "Sovereign Lord, what can you give me since I remain childless and the one who will inherit my estate is Eliezer of Damascus?" And Abram said, "You have given me no children; so a servant in my household will be my heir." Then the word of the Lord came to him: "This man will not be your heir, but a son who is your own flesh and blood will be your heir." He took him outside and said, "Look up at the sky and count the stars—if indeed you can count them." Then he said to him, "So shall your offspring be." Abram believed the Lord, and he credited it to him as righteousness.
(Genesis 15:1-6)

Abram was wealthy in livestock, silver, and gold, yet he had no children. It is recorded that he was about one hundred years old, and Sarah, his wife, was about ninety years old. They were well past their childbearing years. Yet, they longed for a child. God had him look up into the night sky to imagine how numerous his offspring of generations to come would be. This seemed like an impossible feat. Abraham is known for being a man of great faith; however, he was discouraged knowing how old he and Sarah were, so God counted his belief in the promise as faith. Notice how the passage says Abraham believed, but does not record his words. This is worth noting because no matter what we say, God knows what we believe in our hearts. We cannot hide our thoughts, beliefs, or disbeliefs from him. The Lord searches the heart of man and knows how he feels and what he is thinking.

Back to the bride and groom. Remember that the bride and groom have been fasting since the Mikveh bath the day before their wedding. During the wedding ceremony, they shared a glass of wine. Immediately following the ceremony, they are to spend time in seclusion in the Yichud for some privacy as they seal the covenant of marriage.

Imagine the tent set up away from the ceremony, about the distance of a long walk. Imagine the tent made of rich-colored fabrics and adorned with tassels. The overall look is regal and plush. Inside the tent are ornate pillows and covers that are rich in texture. Candles rim the outer area, and a table is set with sweet treats and their favorite delicacies. Another cup of wine is set out for them to share. You can imagine how a time to rest and to have privacy with your groom would be welcomed.

God created sex for marriage. It was created to be an exclusive intimate act one shares in marriage. It is a beautiful way for a husband and wife to express their feelings of love for one another. Sex is an intimate act that binds man and woman together as one flesh and is an expression of commitment to one another. As a couple becomes vulnerable to one another through the act of physical intimacy, God has designed sex to be within the marriage covenant to protect us and bless us. God created physical intimacy so that we can draw close to a person and experience a deep connection in an enjoyable way. Sex within these boundaries remains safe, beautiful, and untainted. It is a bond that carries a husband and wife through years of partnership that is unique from any other relationship. God created sex for this purpose. This is how he planned it to be used, and this is how we benefit.

Chapter 6 Questions

1. Which Jewish wedding tradition did you enjoy?

2. Have do you feel about the man taking all the initiative in the proposal, signing the wedding contract, the Ketubah, and so on?

3. Do you believe God is pursuing you?

7

The Elements

*I betroth you to me forever, I will betroth you in righteousness
and justice, in love and compassion.
(Hosea 2:19)*

According to the Torah, the wedding is a two-part ceremony. Before the
bride and groom have their wedding, there is a ceremony which is very
important: The Kiddush.

Blessing of the Wine, the Kiddush

Blessed are you, Adonai our God, Ruler of the Universe who created the
fruit of the vine.

The Kiddush is a type of betrothal. It is the legal and personal relationship
that exists between a man and a woman. This part of the ceremony could
be written and signed up to a year before the wedding day. This is basically
the engagement part of the relationship but with greater significance. This
is the beginning of a legally binding marriage covenant. However, it is not
the beginning of the bride and groom living together as husband and wife.
This is the old way of doing things.

The father of the bride and the groom have agreed upon the bride
price or the Mohar. The Ketubah, the wedding contract, may either
be written up and signed by the groom on site or it is done later. The
Kiddush was presented during the marriage proposal to the bride. On
a table, between the bride and groom, sits a single cup of wine. If she

accepts the proposal, she will drink from the cup of wine. This signifies her acceptance of the proposal. The cup of wine signifies the Jewish faith's cup of joy. In the very old traditions of this faith, the bride will be busy for the next year preparing for the wedding, and the groom will be building their new home. Now if something were to change with the groom, such as a death or a request for a divorce, the bride would be taken care of according to what is written in the Ketubah. The Kiddush can be done in the beginning of the more modern Jewish wedding ceremony. This places the importance of the wine at the beginning of the ceremony. The cup of wine is a reminder to the Jewish people they are God's chosen people. It is the shared drinking from the cup which is significant. The wine will be blessed before the rest of the ceremony; then the Nissuin follows.

Being fruitful is important to produce wine and to produce a nation. It takes roughly 2.4 pounds of grapes to make a bottle of wine. That's a lot of grapes for one bottle. Remember Abraham, the father of the faith, was promised offspring as numerous as the stars in the heavens. That is a lot of fruitfulness!

We know wine is made from the grapevine, and the definition of fruitful is "yielding and producing fruit, or conducive to an abundant yield, abundantly productive." Maybe this is already obvious: the inclusion of the cup of wine in the wedding ceremony ties to the promise God made to Abraham concerning the inheritance of his ancestors. This is a promise of abundant production and abundant yield.

Imagine Abraham listening to God's promise that his offspring shall be as vast as the stars in the sky. At this point, he and Sarah had given up on the idea of bearing children. Her womb was fruitless. At the age of eighty or ninety, her reproductive system had dried up like a grape that shrinks to a raisin. By providing Abraham and Sarah with Isaac, God demonstrated his abundant power, provision, compassion, and glory. The cup of wine symbolizes faith in God and fellowship with him; this is an important part of the marriage ceremony.

God's Promise

The Jewish faith sees the covenant of marriage like the promise from God to Israel. The Ketubah echoes the covenant promise of God to Israel. The Ketubah was originally initiated at the time of the engagement. It is a legally binding agreement. This is like our American tradition in which we consider the wedding vows to be the binding part of the marriage. As said earlier, the Ketubah could be signed up to a year ahead of the actual marriage ceremony.

Since the ancient Jewish tradition does not recite vows during the Nissuin ceremony, it is the placing of the ring on the finger that finalizes the marriage ceremony. The rabbi may now impart some words of blessing and wisdom.

God's People and the Covenant

> *"But I will establish my covenant with you.."*
> *(Genesis 6:18a)*
>
> *"Behold, I establish my covenant with you and your offspring after you,"*
> *(Genesis 9:9)*
>
> *This is the sign of the covenant I am making between me and you and every living creature with you, a covenant for all generations to come.*
> *(Genesis 9:12)*

The New Testament Church calls itself the bride of Christ because it is referred to as such throughout the New Testament scripture. The idea of the nation of Israel being the bride of God was spoken of often in the Old Testament. There are many references in the writing of the prophets that use this. We know the scriptures can point forward prophetically, and at other times teach an underlying truth. When Jesus taught parables, He consistently referenced the bride, the bridegroom, and the banquet feast.

The Jewish people have covenant weddings, just as God made covenants with them throughout the Old Testament. As God pursued the Jewish nation of Israel, so should a man pursue a woman. The groom invites the bride into the relationship. He then makes promises to care for her in the Ketubah. The groom escorts the bride in the Huppah and places the ring on her finger. The groom breaks the wine glass at the end of the ceremony, symbolically sealing the covenant. The bride simply receives all the action, protection, and benefits.

Who took the initiative to invite you to live with him eternally? Who died on the cross and shed blood to seal the covenant of this invitation? Covenants were first established in Genesis, when God made a commitment to his creation and Israel. God's words in Genesis demonstrate his intent toward mankind and his creation. Covenants are important. They are used for a greater purpose. God used them to show his unconditional love toward man and his faithfulness to us. He knew that we were sinners and we would turn away from him. He knew that we were incapable of living faithfully. But God is faithful. God never turns from us. He made these covenants to demonstrate his love under all conditions. He made these covenants to demonstrate that he can fulfill what man's power cannot.

Thus, the marriage covenant echoes his unconditional love. We all know that a married couple will disappoint each other. We know that to love unconditionally, every day, is difficult. God has modeled this for us and wants us to call on him to achieve and sustain this unconditional love. I am not promoting an unhealthy love. That is not biblical. Faithfulness and unconditional love should never fall into the realm of an abusive relationship.

My husband and I did not have a covenant marriage. We were not believers until three years into our marriage. Years later, we had a quiet ceremony and made a new covenant with one another. I am thankful that we still enjoy one another and have remained within the covenant.

The Abrahamic Covenant

> *I will make you into a great nation, and I will bless you; I*
> *will make your name great, and you will be a blessing. I will*
> *bless those who bless you, and whoever curses you I will curse;*
> *and all peoples on earth will be blessed through you.*
> *(Genesis 12:2-3)*

There are five blessings in those two verses. God is big on blessing his people through covenants. That should reason enough to want a covenant marriage.

God is in the business of blessing. He is a generous God, and it is in his nature to bless. Having a marriage that is centered on God will be a blessing to you. Having a heart that is centered on God's purpose will bless you. Having faith like Abraham will bless you. God's love holds no bounds when we look at what he did on the cross. God's love and blessings hold no bounds to the impossible things he did for Abraham, and he will do the same for you. The God of the Old Testament is the God of the New Testament. When I started to encounter God on a personal level, I witnessed what he could do for me. I experienced how much he loved me, how majestic he was, and I couldn't help but pursue him more. I wanted to know his love more—more answers to prayers and more of his presence in my life.

> *For nothing will be impossible with God.*
> *(Luke 1:37)*

God does the impossible. He took an elderly couple who was childless and made a great nation. Here is another situation. Reference the above scripture. Angels wait on God in his courts, and you can be sure they know his power and witness it daily. What impossible news did the angels tell Mary? They told her she was going to have a child.

We see that God oversees all creation. He made it possible for Abraham and Sarah to have a child, and their offspring would multiply into a great nation. He made it possible through the power of the Holy Spirit for Mary, a virgin, to give birth to the Messiah of the world. Now, do you wonder what impossible things God is going to make possible for your marriage and life? Remember, all things are possible with God!

How Is a Covenant Sealed?

Sometimes a covenant can be sealed over a meal, a handshake, or with a written formal document. The highest level is sealed with the shedding of blood. Abraham's covenant with God was sealed through the shedding of blood. The physical act of intimacy between a man and woman in some cultures and traditions is considered a covenant confirming a legal marriage.

Our Cup of Joy

> In the same way, after the supper he took the cup, saying, "This cup is the new covenant in my blood, which is poured out for you."
> (Luke 22:20)

Jesus is our cup of joy. He is the Lamb of God, the perfect sacrifice for our sins, and was prepared to offer himself up for a permanent covenant made with his blood. Peter, his disciple, soon after hearing what Jesus said at the Last Supper, took things into his own hands. At the Garden of Gethsemane, Peter stepped forward to protect Christ.

> Then Simon Peter, who had a sword, drew it and struck the high priest's servant, cutting off his right ear. (The servant's name was Malchus.) Jesus commanded Peter, "Put your sword away! Shall I not drink the cup the Father has given me?"
> (John 18:10-11)

Jesus's reply ties together the covenant cup symbolized in the ancient Jewish wedding with the purpose of why he became man and lived among us. It is through the covenant cup that Christ seals our relationship through his suffering on the cross.

The Garden of Gethsemane is one of my favorite passages to read. It always causes me to pause and reflect on how painful it was for Christ to take on my sin. Beforehand, he was suffering to the point of sweating blood because he knew the horrible pain of the cross and that taking our sin upon himself would bring separation between him and his Father. Sin separates us from the presence of God. God hates sin and darkness but loves the sinner. God is light and holiness. Darkness and light cannot coexist.

> *He withdrew about a stone's throw beyond them, knelt down and prayed, "Father, if you are willing, take this cup from me; yet not my will, but yours be done." An angel from heaven appeared to him and strengthened him. And being in anguish, he prayed more earnestly, and his sweat was like drops of blood falling to the ground.*
> *(Luke 22:41-44)*

Jesus accepted the pain of the cross because of his love for us. He was obedient to his Father's plan. In the end it would be counted as his cup of joy. It is through his suffering, that we are cleansed. We are lifted from the darkness of our sins. It is because he rises from the dead that our sorrow will turn to joy.

> *"Very truly I tell you, you will weep and mourn while the world rejoices. You will grieve, but your grief will turn to joy."*
> *(John 16:20)*

Here is a poem I wrote about suffering. It has helped me view suffering as the scripture above explains. Our suffering will be turned to joy.

SUFFERING

Oh, to suffer without complaint.
Do we see it as a burst of joy?
Light ever bright on the other side.
Will it spark like a star, an exchange in Thy Kingdom,
Shining brightly at His feet for us to see?
Our pain now, not darkness or despair,

But a life of light we lay there.
Transformed the former in a translation of brilliance,
Will be a crown we cast to our king?
Must I then welcome but not hunger for this stain cast upon my flesh,
Coating my emotions, striating my bones,
Just to get a glimpse further of His abundant light?
Oh, that I may see and feel and be aligned with His bloodshed wounds,
And be transported into His presence, permitted rest,
Indwelled with the hope of His beauty.
May I suffer without despair.
His promises to coat my moaning,
His light to me moving,
His present love to carry me to the day,
He will touch my face.
Such intimacy I desire.
He will lay his wounded hands
Upon my yet untransformed afflicted face,
And all of today's suffering will burst forth with His brilliance,
Over with a clap of thunder.
There, reigning in His presence,
His glorious encapsulating presence!
No darkness, no despair, no heaviness of heart.
No more bent over sorrow!
Yet, the One who lit the world has set me upon a soft landing,
Into His arms, inseparable from His joy.
Gloriously filled, gloriously healed, gloriously indwelled!
His presence prevails!

The Nissuin:
The Second Part of the Ceremony

Blessed are you, Adonai our God, Ruler of the Universe who created the fruit of the vine.

The Nissuin begins after the blessing of the wine, which is traditionally poured. Then the seven blessings are read, followed by the giving of the ring, the reading of the Ketubah, the second glass of wine, and the breaking of the glass. The giving of the ring is done by the groom. We will talk in more detail about this later. The order of these events can vary according to region and time in history.

The Sheva Brachot:
The Seven Blessings

There are seven blessings spoken during the Nissuin. It is interesting only one of the seven blessings are about the bride and groom. The couple is declaring that their marriage has a higher purpose than satisfying their own needs and desires.

1. Blessed are you, Adonai our God, Ruler of the Universe, who created everything for Your glory.
2. Blessed are you, Adonai our God, Ruler of the Universe, creator of man.
3. Blessed are you, Adonai our God, Ruler of the Universe, who created man in His image, in the pattern of His own likeness, and provided for the perpetuation of his kind. Blessed are You, Adonai, shaper of humanity.
4. May the barren one exalt and be glad as her children are joyfully gathered to her. Blessed are you, Adonai, who gladdened Zion with her children.
5. Grant great joy to these loving companions as You once gladdened your creations in the Garden of Eden. Blessed are You, Adonai, who gladdened the bridegroom and the bride.

6. Blessed are Thou Lord, our God, King of the universe, who created joy and gladness, groom and bride, rejoicing, glad song, pleasure, delight, love, brotherhood, peace, and companionship. Soon, Lord our God, let there be heard in the cities of Judah and in the streets of Jerusalem the sound of joy and the sound of gladness, the voice of the groom and the voice of the bride, the sound of jubilation of grooms from their canopies and of the youths from their feasts of song. Blessed art thou, LORD, Who gladdens the groom with the bride.

7. Blessed are Thou Lord our God, King of the universe, Creator of the fruit of the vine.

The Breaking of the Glass

Mazel Tov!

Mazel Tov is a Jewish expression of congratulations or good luck.

The wedding ceremony ends with a loud noise. The groom stomps the wine glass, crushing it into tiny pieces. This breaking of the glass signifies that the ceremony is complete and the wedding feast may begin. As the glass is broken, everyone will shout, "Mazel Tov!" The celebration begins.

People seem most curious about the reason behind the breaking of the glass in the Jewish tradition. After some research, I found many of the reasons tie back to the persecution of the Jewish people. As joyful and celebratory as this moment appears, the sobriety of their suffering is never to be forgotten.

Here are some explanations about the breaking of the glass:

1. The breaking of the glass is a reminder of the destruction of the temple.
2. It demonstrates the husband's authority.
3. It demonstrates the frailty of love in marriage. This is a warning to be careful in how you treat one another because it can be difficult to put a marriage back together.

4. The shattered glass is a reminder that although the wedding has provided a taste of redemption, the world is in exile, broken and requiring our care.
5. This tradition is a reminder of the time during the Holocaust when all the windows of Jewish businesses and home, and all things of value, were broken.
6. It is a reminder that there will be tough times ahead.
7. The women make a joke that it is the last time the husband puts his foot down (this is my favorite, Mazel Tov!)

Sacrifices, Circumcision, and the Broken Glass

Examples of cutting in the Old Testament are common. The animals were cut to make a sacrifice according to the specifications of the Mosaic Law. The covenant between Abraham and God in Genesis 17 was done through circumcision, the cutting of the flesh. The Ten Commandments were broken. The woman's body was designed to show the cut of the sealing of the marriage covenant when they first lay together. The shattering of the wine glass represents all of these. As believers we see, Christ was crucified and was the final blood sacrifice for us. The details of the ancient Jewish wedding traditions continue to echo his plan of redemption. God's fingerprints are all around us and all throughout our lives, continually pointing to his Word and his plan to redeem mankind. He has not stood back and neglected his pursuit of us. We are his creation, and he wants us to be with him forever.

Remember that the curtain of the temple separated man from the Tabernacle. Only the high priest was allowed through there once a year at Yom Kippur.

> *Therefore, if anyone is in Christ, the new creation has come:*
> *The old has gone, the new is here!*
> *(2 Corinthians 5:17)*

After Christ died, the curtain tore in two. This is the new way; the old is gone. We now have full access to Jesus. No man needs to mediate between God and us. The veil was cut, torn, and the new covenant fulfilled!

The bride and groom have full access to one another. See how this echoes our relationship with Christ? Under the new covenant with Christ, we have an intimate relationship. God has broken through all our barriers, and we are now allowed to know him personally. Just as a husband and wife know one another, this relationship echoes God's love for us. If people are honest, they will tell you that the best of marriages is never perfect. We practice a lot of forgiveness, grace, and mercy in our marital relationships. But God's love is perfect. He is the Father and Creator of forgiveness, grace, and mercy. Marriage is a gift and a blessing from God It is a glimpse of his desire for a relationship with us. It allows us to see how patient God is with us as he loves us unconditionally. Remember that God's love is perfect, constant, and it never changes.

Jesus Christ is the same yesterday, today, and forever.
(Hebrews 13:8)

Chapter 7 Questions

1. Which of these wedding traditions did you enjoy? Why?

2. What do you understand so far concerning the wine and Jesus suffering on the cross?

3. How has your understanding concerning 'covenant' increased?

8

Our Traditions

Jesus and Martha

> *Jesus said to her, "I am the resurrection and the life. The one who believes in me will live, even though they die; and whoever lives by believing in me will never die. Do you believe this?"*
> *(John 11:25-26)*

When Jesus saw Martha, he declared himself as God to her and asked for a response. This was right before he raised her brother Lazarus from the dead, one of his greatest miracles. Maybe she was doubting Jesus because her brother died. Take note, he asked her if she believed in him before he performed the miracle of raising her brother Lazarus. Martha did not know he was going to raise him. Will you believe in Christ if you do not witness a miracle in your lifetime? Will you believe in Christ if your loved ones suffer to the point of death? He is asking for a response from all of us. Many people are noted to have faith even as their lives did not go well. Is the reason you believe in Christ because you know the depravity of your sin and you know that you need his life exchanged for your wretchedness? Have you sustained from cheapening the grace of God by not turning his blessings into the prosperity gospel? Do you pray, "Thy will be done," even as the stakes are high?

How does Martha answer? In John 11:27, "Yes, Lord, I have believed that you are the Christ." This statement means that she believes that Christ is the Messiah for whom the Jewish faith has been waiting. She continues with, "The Son of God." She is stating she believes he is begotten by God and thus is God. Last, she states, "Even he who comes into the world." She acknowledges he has come down from his heavenly court and taken on human form. Martha believes Jesus was and is God before he came to be born of man, the eternal God.

By the time Jesus arrived at the tomb, it had been four days since Lazarus's death. Jesus asked for the stone to be removed so he could enter the cave. Martha replied, "Lord, by this time there will be a stench, for he has been dead already four days." She reminded him how strong and offensive bodily odors of the dead could overwhelm him. Maybe she was just nervous about what was ahead and was trying to avoid the emotions.

In verse 40 Jesus replied, "Did I not say to you that if you believe, you will see the glory of God?" Note that these are not the exact words he used earlier. Jesus exchanged the words, "I am the resurrection and the life," for, "You will see the glory of God." This is the exchange; what he did at the resurrection of the cross for us, how we can see his glory. Of all the miracles Christ did, his resurrection, the conquering of our death, has allowed us to see his glory. He took what did not belong to him, our sin, upon himself, and exchanged it for his holiness. He took the wrath headed toward all mankind, the weight of sin was about to drown us into the sorrow of eternity, and he cast it off by giving his life.

Do you believe in the resurrection of life?
Did you answer, "I do," to your divine groom?
Do you profess Jesus is the resurrected life who died for our sins?
Do you believe he is the Son of God?
Do you believe he came into this world from on high?
Are you willing to follow him as he has called you to do?
If you answered I do to the above questions, then eternal life can be yours.
The altar you are standing at is the foot of the cross looking over at the empty tomb. As you say, "I do," to him, you enter his Kingdom for eternity.
We stop the story here, although it has a happy ending. But stopping it here is important. Are you willing to follow Christ if your life continues

to be a struggle? If life does not go well, but you still have the comfort of Christ? The question is this: Is the resurrection, the promise of eternal life, and the presence of the Holy Spirit enough?

People who know me know that I am passionate about prayer. Yet, I am challenged to stop myself and ask, "If God did not answer another prayer in my lifetime, is the resurrection and the comfort of the Holy Spirit enough?"

We live in such abundance here in the United States, is the work of the cross and the presence of the Holy Spirit enough? It can be easy to work out our lives, in our strength, forgetting the power available through God and missing the point of our life.

After Jesus saw Lazarus, he wept. Jesus feels all our pain. He came here and experienced the depravity of mankind. Sin shot out the gate, and in Genesis 4, murder took its presence on earth. When he walked the earth, he experienced the brokenness of mankind. He did not live isolated from pain. His cousin, John the Baptist, was beheaded. He saw the cripples, lepers, the blind, the broken, the hardhearted. Jesus experienced loss, sorrow, loneliness, betrayal, and hatred. He loved Lazarus and was moved by the love of his family and friends.

Martha still did not know Jesus was going to raise Lazarus. Many of our stories end here, and the physical healing doesn't come. The loved one is not resurrected. I know the pain from sickness; my baby sister died several years ago. Jesus is a miracle worker, and the Holy Spirit sustains us through pain and turmoil. But my Jesus is the resurrected Jesus. I said, "I do," at the cross. The exchange of my sins for eternal life is enough, no matter what is ahead for me. How about you? Will you say, "I do," to Jesus as he works out his will in your life, no matter the outcome?

The Traditional Wedding Ceremony

Moving on to the American traditions, we have another perspective. This ceremony is based on vows, promises by both the bride and groom.

"I, _____, take thee,_____, to be my wedded wife/husband to have and to hold, from this day forward, for better, for worse, for richer, for poorer, in sickness and health, to love and to cherish, till death do us part, according to God's holy ordinance, and thereto I pledge my faith to you."

There are many variations of the above vows. Some words are interchanged to, "honor and obey," "this is a solemn vow, forsaking all others," and "in good times and bad." These are all examples of different traditions. The words, "I do," "promise," or "covenant" are included. Today, many couples like to rewrite the vows to personalize them according to their own beliefs. Marriage vows are important and should be taken with the intent to fulfill them. A promise is a promise.

The simple words, "I do," are magical. We love to hear the bride and groom say them to one another. Two simple words and three letters make a lifelong promise. In a marriage, two people commit to one another, and the story of their joined life begins.

Jesus is committed to us. In the Old Testament, the Ark of the Covenant, where the presence of God resided, was transported through the desert with the Israelites carrying these words from Deuteronomy 3:6–8 inside it: "I will not forsake you." God repeats himself when he wants to make sure we understand him. He is committed to us. He loves us unconditionally.

The Wedding Certificate and the Book of Life

At the end of the wedding ceremony in American culture, a wedding certificate is signed. This legally binds a couple. There are usually two witnesses who must attest to this truth, as well as the signature of the one who performed the ceremony. In the ancient Jewish tradition, the Ketubah is signed only by the groom and the two witnesses present.

The one who is victorious will, like them, be dressed in white. I will never blot out the name of that person from the book of life, but will acknowledge that name before my Father and his angels.
(Revelation 3:5)

When you say yes to Christ, you have given your life to him, you are adopted into God's family, and thus your name is written in the Book of Life. If you have an adopted a child, you realize how important the final paper work is which states you are the child's parent. I have three biological children and one adopted daughter, Sophie. For an adopted child the final paperwork that you receive stating you are the child's parent is very important. One of the reasons for its importance derives from the difficulty to replace it and there is no DNA test to prove you are the parent. We keep our children's birth certificates in a safe place but take special care with Sophie's. It is through the blood of Christ allowing us to be grafted into his family. Make no mistake: we belong to his family when we say yes to Christ.

Another Story

When our daughter was adopted from China, we had some difficulty. It gave new meaning to the words "red tape." I won't go into the backstory but let me say the adoption took longer than usual. I worried about her and whether they were caring for her properly and feeding her enough, and I began to wonder if we were ever going to bring her home.

We had a very cute picture of her on our refrigerator with a bright red background. I would tell anyone who came to visit, this was the daughter we were waiting to bring home. I believe this is similar to how God views us. It is like he has our pictures hanging up while waiting for us to respond to his request to adopt us, his invitation to "Come follow me." Then he takes them down and places them in his family album titled, *The Book of Life.*

When my husband arrived in China, it took three days to straighten out the paperwork. Finally, they told him to come down to the lobby of the White Swan Hotel to receive her at 6:00 p.m. My husband never wears a tie without an ultimatum from me. But on this special day, he put on a tie, set up a video camera in the room, and recorded the moment. It went something like this: "Sophia, I am your daddy, and I am going to come down right now to adopt you and to receive you into our family. You will now be one of us." This is just like how God does it. As God adopts us, it is announced in heaven, the angels sing, the Holy Spirit descends upon us, and we are received into his family.

The next day, after my husband received Sophia, I flew in to find her sleeping on down pillows with fists full of food in each hand. She was content with us, complete strangers because somehow, she knew this was her new family!

Is your name written in the Book of Life?

When our daughter was about ten years old and she was asked about her faith, and she knew the answer, "I was adopted twice. Once by my parents, and then by God."

Chapter 8 Questions

1. Which of the American traditions did you most enjoy reading about?

2. What is your understanding so far of the concept of the vow ceremony relating to your relationship with Jesus?

3. What questions do you have so far concerning what you have learned? If there is a question about your faith, how are you going to get the answers?

9

The Right Hand and the Ring

The Melding of Two Lives

A few years ago, I went to the wedding of a young couple. The bride had held to a commitment of purity. For many years, she wore a purity ring as a reminder. During the wedding, she presented her husband with his wedding ring made from the melting of her purity ring into his new ring.

Living a life of purity means that Satan does not control that part of you. It states that you understand the holiness of your God and are seeking it. A marriage started on this foundation will be built upon the rock of Jesus Christ. This foundation will bless you. The Lord's right hand will be over you, protecting you and leading you. The Lord's right hand will sustain you through life. Meld your life and marriage into God's hands. Blessings!

Left or Right
Story of the Prodigal Son
Luke 15

In the book *The Return of the Prodigal Son* by Henri Nouwen, he talks about Rembrandt's painting *The Lost Son* which is about the story in Luke 15. Rembrandt's *The Lost Son* depicts God and who we are in him. The details of this painting are the story of the hands of the father symbolizing the hands of God. The complexities of his painted hands articulate the depth of God, his love for us, and the balance of his character between the juxtaposition of left hand and right hand. Creator God tenderly holding, yet firmly gripping. He draws to turn toward him, to repentance, yet holding us so tenderly becoming vulnerable.

Left Hand

The left hand is soft, resting gently on the son's shoulder. This hand transports God's love, resting on us, assuring of our safety in him. It is the soft touch that says, "I am here with you, for you, and we are together in this life. The Father's hand says, "Rest in me; I have your life covered; my yoke is easy. I am carrying your burdens; rest in me; I am with you." This is the hand of compassion and unconditional love that brings us to repentance, drawing us forward to continue to seek knowing him.

The left hand is the one that turns you back to the Father as you have detoured onto the crossroad of regrets. This hand of God points us back to the soft place in his arms, restoring wayward children. Yes, you may have traveled up and down this road many times. God is not counting your travel miles. The trail may be covered with your foot prints of delusion from wrong living, but he is there, running toward you, calling your name. His eyes searching the vast horizon. He is looking for you to come home to him, eager for a glimpse of his child's appearance, the one he loves and yearns to hold in order to restore him from the wears of life.

The left hand brings us to our knees as we see the depth of our sins and the provision that restores us to him.

The Right Hand

The right hand is the one which holds the sign that says, "Danger ahead. Stop. Turn." The right hand depicts the firm grip of God. He will never let you go. He will never forsake you. This is the Father's firm hand which holds his child up, lifts the child after he falls. The hand holding his Word so that we can reflect upon it and be strengthened and straightened in our walking and living. The hand holding you close under his wings of protection as the winds of life try to sweep you away. You may feel the storm moving you east or west, but he has a grip on your cloak and firmly establishes you.

The right hand is set over creation. It holds all things together, moves the moon and the sun into place, sets the ocean and seas boundary line. This is the hand moving into action, giving you a way out as you tilt toward a wayward crossroad. This is the hand shielding you as evil tendrils reach for you.

His unconditional love, does not point to our dark past, but pushes us forward to the loving embrace, reminding us of his holiness. It is in our desire for his holy presence as we clasp his hands allowing them to cover us, bowing our heads breathing in his perfect way. Like *The Lost Son*, we kneel in the presence of a loving God who blankets us with unconditional love and takes us into his arms without a second's hesitation. He sets upon us like a favorite old warm coat, holding us close. God is there, clasping us with each hand: the left and the right together in a perfect balance of authority and compassion, safety and provision, upholding and comforting.

His left and right hand were both tied to the cross, enduring the nails, taking our pain so that we may go free and find our way home to our Father. As the Father looks down the long, decrepit road at his prodigal lost children, Jesus looked down on his sons and daughters from the cross, inviting them to return and find their way home to the Father through Him. He is the way! The invitation to come to God is written by his left hand of compassion and forgiveness, and his right hand of firmness holding us steady until we are in his presence. May you grasp both of God's hands and never leave his care.

There is an old gospel song, "Two Coats," about an old coat, tattered, and torn, and a new coat which has never been worn. The writer asks his master what must he do? The refrain is, "I'll tell you the best thing I ever did do, I took off the old coat and put on the new." There is new way in Christ! A new way to live! Take off the old coat, and put on the new.

> *Show me the wonders of your great love, you who save by your right hand those who take refuge in you from their foes. (Psalm 17:7)*

The right hand is a common theme across all wedding traditions. Shall the ring be placed on the left hand or the right? Apparently, this question has a different answer depending on the country, region, and religion you claim.

It is said that the third finger on the left hand is considered the closest to the heart because the vein on this hand runs directly to the heart. Because of this, the tradition of the right hand was moved to the left hand in some cultures. It is called the vein of love.

> *For I am the Lord your God who takes hold of your right hand and says to you, "Do not fear; I will help you." (Isaiah 41:13)*

The Latin translation for the word *left* is "sinistris," which is where we get the word *sinister*. The Latin translation for the word *right* is "dextris," which is where we get the word *dexter*. There has been at times a superstition if you were left-handed, it was a mark of evil. Plus, there are all the phrases that go along with the word right: "Get on the right side of your boss," "Let's be on the right side," "He is not right-minded."

Years ago, there was even a practice used by school teachers and mothers to tie the left hand behind the back of left-handed child's, forcing them to use their right hand. This could be traumatizing to a child. I had a friend who was left-handed and had experienced having her left hand tied back during her early education. To this day, she cannot keep her left and right directions straight. When she drives, she gets confused. If her coworkers ask her to get something on her left side, she will reach to her right. In good humor, they say to her, "No, your other left hand."

God's Powerful Right Hand and the Ring

During the wedding ceremony, the pastor may ask the bride and groom to face one another and clasp their right hands together. This is the traditional way that American weddings are set up to exchange vows.

The dominance of the right hand is seen through much of scripture.

*Even there your hand will guide me, your right hand will
hold me fast.*
(Psalm 139:10)

*And so he brought them to the border of this holy land, to the
hill country his right hand had taken.*
(Psalm 78:54)

The root your right hand has planted.
(Psalm 80:15a)

*Show the wonders of your great love, you who save by your
right hand those who take refuge in you from their foes.*
(Psalm 17:7)

*In your majesty ride forth victoriously in the cause of truth,
humility and justice; let your right hand achieve awesome deeds.*
(Psalm 45:4)

*You make known to me the path of life; in your presence there
is fullness of joy; at your right hand are pleasures forevermore.*
(Psalm 16:11)

*But when this priest had offered for all time one sacrifice for
sins, he sat down at the right hand of God.*
(Hebrews 10:12)

In the ancient Jewish wedding, the ring is placed on the bride's right hand. The groom does not receive a ring during the ceremony. The ring does not have any stones in it so there is no question of its value. Since the groom takes all the initiative in the ceremony he places the ring on the bride's finger as he says,

"You are consecrated to me through this ring, in accordance with the religion of Moses and Israel."

The word consecrated means "to make holy." It is through Christ on the cross that we are made holy.

In every part of the wedding ceremony, the words of blessings and promises tie back to the Jewish faith. As believers in Jesus Christ, we see how God has drawn us forward to him through the wedding ceremony and this covenant relationship between a husband and wife.

One obvious thing about this ring is its shape. The circular form reminds us of eternity with no beginning or end. The hole in the center of it has been compared to a door or gateway to pass into or through. Here the gospel of entering through Christ is echoed.

What Are You Going to Do?

What are you going to do with this gentleman named Jesus who holds out his right hand for you to grasp and hold? He wants to hold you, protect you, lead you, and provide for you. Will you grasp it and join him into eternal life?

Chapter 9 Questions

1. For you personally, what is the significance of the wedding ring?

2. How have you responded to Jesus inviting you into a relationship?

3. Do you see Jesus as gently pursing you, or a more diligent pursuit? Or both?

10

The Bread

Hamotzi: The Blessing of the Bread
The Wedding Banquet

Double Portions
When they had crossed, Elijah said to Elisha, "Tell me, what can I do for you before I am taken from you?" "Let me inherit a double portion of your spirit," Elisha replied.
(2 Kings 2:9)

Before I compare this tradition to our spiritual lives, I must tell a mom story. Our daughter, Paige, was a very picky eater. I used to tease her, telling her that she would go to her high school prom ordering chicken nuggets while sitting in a fancy restaurant. Years ago, some friends watched our kids for the weekend. They took them out to a pizza buffet. Before then, Paige did not eat pizza. However, she was either embarrassed, or just hungry. We found out after the weekend, she ate lots of pizza. She loved it. The next time we had a family night and ordered pizza, she grabbed double portions!

I really love the above verse. First, we can see there was something about the way Elijah lived and followed God that impressed Elisha. He had been watching him for some time. Before Elijah was taken to heaven, Elisha asked for a double portion of God's spirit. He saw that the spirit on Elijah was good, and he asked for more.

As I thought about this, I decided to apply this to my prayer life. Occasionally, I will remember this and pray it with enthusiasm. It thrills me to ask for double portions. I love to do this while praying for someone else. Can you imagine having someone pray double portions over you? There is no end to his power, provision, love, and forgiveness. Why not ask for double portions of blessings?

Hamotzi: The Blessing of the Bread

> *Put the bread of the Presence on this table to be before me*
> *at all times.*
> *(Exodus 25:30)*
>
> *This bread is to be set out before the Lord regularly, Sabbath*
> *after Sabbath, on the behalf of the Israelites, as a lasting*
> *covenant.*
> *(Leviticus 24:8)*

The bread of the presence represents God's everlasting provision, a promise made in a covenant with his people. This bread, twelve loaves, was set in the Tabernacle and made fresh daily. It was a memorial bread set out as an offering with the oil of frankincense sprinkled on it.

God provided daily bread, manna, for Israel in the desert. He provided bread for King David as he ran from Saul, and he provided bread for Christ as he fed the five thousand. You can see that God continues to stay consistent in the elements he uses to redeem man, supplicate him, and celebrate life. Bread is another one of these elements that, like the vineyard, the blood covenants, and the water, are tethered together to draw man to the redemption table. Then, as we come to the Last Supper, we see Jesus brings forth all the elements to point to the answer found on the cross.

> *While they were eating, Jesus took bread, and when he had*
> *given thanks, he broke it and gave it to his disciples, saying,*
> *"Take and eat; this is my body."*
> *(Matthew 26:26)*

The bread represents the covenant of Christ's body broken for us and his provision to meet our daily needs and our eternal need of replacing our depravity with his holiness.

Greeting the Guests

The receiving line in the traditional American wedding is a formal way for the bride, groom, and immediate family to greet guests after the ceremony. Though it isn't as common today, this tradition's purpose is to give the guests a chance to bestow their best wishes to the newly married couple. The blessing of the bread in the ancient Jewish faith, is this: "Blessed are you Adonai, Ruler of the Universe, who brings bread from the earth."

The blessing of the bread is the first blessing said at the reception before the meal begins. After the bread is blessed, the bride and groom walk around and place a loaf on each table. This practice gives them the opportunity to greet their guests one by one. The bread is braided in a manner that allows the rolls to sit side by side. The bread is first covered on top and bottom with a cloth, representing the dew of the manna bread.

> The people of Israel called the bread manna. It was white like coriander seed and tasted like wafers made with honey. (Exodus 16:31)

The bread appears to be a mound like rolls set in a side-by-side manner. There are two reasons for this. First, to remind us of God's double portions, and second, to represent both our part and God's part in his divine plan. Though our part is not equal to God's, we have the privilege of being used by him within his plan for creation.

A knife would be hidden next to the bread, though it will never be used. This shows that we only need what God provides to live. The knife symbolizes mankind's trying to cut into what God is doing. Only gentle fingers are needed to pull a portion off the loaf and to pass it to the next person. The bread is prepared with our hands and eaten with our hands. When it comes to God's blessings, you do not need anything the world gives you.

Know this: We are saved by grace, God's unmerited favor. No matter what we do once we know Christ, he will not forsake us. Christ loves us with an everlasting love, and that is all we need. There are benefits to seeking him while getting to know his power and majesty. He is our helper. Just as the groom initiates all things in drawing his bride to himself, so God draws us to himself. We are invited to work alongside God because the fields are ready for harvesting, and he would like our help. This is an invitation to work with God.

> *Then he said to his disciples, "The harvest is plentiful but the workers are few."*
> *(Matthew 9:37)*

Chapter 10 Questions

1. What part of your life would you pray for double portions for?

2. Are you ready to work for God's harvest? Where do you think he has called you?

The Wedding of Cana and the Last Supper

The Changing Water into Wine

Nearby stood six stone water jars, the kind used by the Jews for ceremonial washing, each holding from twenty to thirty gallons. Jesus said to the servants, "Fill the jars with water", so they filled them to the brim.

Then he told them, "Now draw some out and take it to the master of the banquet."

They did so, and the master of the banquet tasted the water that had been turned into wine. He did not realize where it came from, though the servants who had drawn the water knew. Then he called the bridegroom aside and said, "Everyone brings out the choice wine first and then the cheaper wine after the guests have had too much to drink, but you have saved the best till now."

What Jesus did here in Cana of Galilee was the first of the signs through which he revealed his glory; and his disciples believed in him.
(John 2:6–11)

Jesus's first miracle was one of compassion. He covered the shame of the bride and groom and prevented the embarrassment they would face by running out of wine. Because of the significance of wine in an ancient

Jewish wedding, running out of the wine would stop the festivities. It would be an embarrassment. A wedding feast without wine would cause guest to leave early. The tradition of celebrations went on for days, at times it was a week-long celebration.

I love how Jesus had compassion for the bride and groom. I love that Jesus's first miracle was to cover their shame. Isn't that what the cross is all about? Jesus came to cover our shame. I don't know about you, but I am humiliated and ashamed of my sins. I am so thankful Jesus came to cover them and discard them forever.

God is compassionate. "And he passed in front of Moses, proclaiming, 'The Lord, the Lord, the compassionate and gracious God, slow to anger, abounding in love and faithfulness, maintaining love to thousands, and forgiving wickedness, rebellion and sin.'" (Exodus 34:6–7) These words are repeated over and over in the Bible. Is this the God you know: compassionate, gracious, slow to anger, abounding in love and faithfulness, and forgiving of wickedness, rebellion, and sin? Which part of the above list is hard for you to accept?

Hovering Over the Waters

The introduction of the Holy Spirit speaks of it hovering over waters as creation is made. To me, it looks evident water was used as a tool between God and man: to draw him near through baptism, to meet his physical needs, and to reveal the greatness of God by the parting of the sea.

> The earth was without form, and void; and darkness was on the face of the deep. And the Spirit of God was hovering over the face of the waters.
> (Genesis 1:2)

This introduction reminds me of a musician waiting backstage to come out and perform a great overture. In this scripture, the stage is set by God as the Holy Spirit is waiting with great anticipation to be released and to start his magnificent work through water, one of his most significant instruments. Not only did God make water something that comprises about seventy percent of the human body, he made it something that is pleasant to drink, use, and look upon. The Holy Spirit is eager to touch mankind, to release us from our shame, to help us, to quench our thirst spiritually, and to change us from the inside out. As Jesus changes the water into wine, he is ushering in a new way. Christ is here, and things are different now. The old way is out, and the new way is here.

> *Therefore, if anyone is in Christ, he is a new creation. The old has passed away; behold, the new has come.*
> *(2 Corinthians 5:17)*

Follow the water jar. The water has been changed into wine. The jars used for ceremonial cleansing have been changed into the best wine. God wants us to be changed into a new creation. The new way is here!

The God of the Old Testament used water to clear a path to lead people to the Promised Land and lead us to redemption through a new way.

Think of all the Old Testament stories with water: Noah and the Ark, Jonah and the fish, the parting of the Red Sea, Moses hitting a rock to bring forth water, and on the stories go. God worked through water to free people, to redeem mankind, and to rescue a nation.

The Holy Spirit is hovering over you, wanting and waiting to touch you, change you from the inside out, redeem you, wash you clean, and build you up. The Holy Spirit is here to help you let go of your old way of doing things and bring in a new way, one that is best for you.

The God of the Old Testament is here. The God that used water to reach man, rescue him, lead him, and to encounter his majesty is the same God. God is consistent. He has not changed. The Messiah was prophesied, and here the Holy Spirit is, hovering over the water at a wedding. God is the same yesterday, today, and tomorrow.

The idea of the Holy Spirit may be one you shy away from. Do not fear; it has been a difficult one for many to grasp.

> *All this I have spoken while still with you. But the Advocate,*
> *the Holy Spirit, whom the Father will send in my name, will*
> *teach you all things and will remind you of everything I have*
> *said to you."*
> *(John 14:25-26)*

The name of the Holy Spirit is Counselor. The work of the Holy Spirit is many things. One of them is to reveal the depth of Jesus's teachings. It guides us in wisdom and enables us to live the lives that God has planned for us. The Holy Spirit is sent from the Father to verify we belong to him. What is it about the Holy Spirit that you struggle with? Be honest with yourself and ask God to guide your understanding.

The Cleansing Jars

In the book of Leviticus, there are many laws, rules, and instructions. They go into detail about what was clean and unclean to eat. Leviticus outlines the cleansing of infectious skin diseases, how to clean mildew, the cleansing of different types of discharges, and the purification a woman must go through after childbirth. In some ways, it is written like a medical journal. God gave these rules to keep the people safe and healthy.

Over ten chapters are devoted to cleanliness and purity. Uncleanliness was a threat to human life, and some of the laws were written to protect people from falling into sin. The old saying, "Cleanliness is next to godliness," may have taken root here. The original laws dealt with cleanliness and sin. Many manmade laws were added later and became outward performances to demonstrate to those watching how holy they were. For example, there was a procedure to pour a cup of water twice over the right hand and then twice over the left hand that was added by man. During this washing, you were to be careful not to touch one hand to the other, and while drying off the hand, a benediction needed to be recited out loud. This instance demonstrates how man's laws served no purpose. Instead, God's laws protected them from disease, death, and sin.

Jesus's words are straight to the point.

> *"Woe to you, teachers of the law and Pharisees, you hypocrites! You clean the outside of the cup and dish, but inside they are full of greed and self-indulgence. Blind Pharisee! First clean the inside of the cup and dish, and then the outside also will be clean." "Woe to you, teachers of the law and Pharisees, you hypocrites! You are like whitewashed tombs, which look beautiful on the outside but on the inside are full of the bones of the dead and everything unclean."*
> *(Matthew 23:25-27)*

The word hypocrite originally comes from the Greek word "hypokrites", which means "an actor." This gives a deeper meaning to what Jesus is saying, doesn't it? They were doing all the outward actions, but inside they were not seeking God.

> *But the Lord said to Samuel, "Do not consider his appearance or his height, for I have rejected him. The Lord does not look at the things people look at. People look at the outward appearance, but the Lord looks at the heart."*
> *(1 Samuel 16:7)*

I shared earlier that I saw a vision of my heart as a little shriveled black briquette. I needed to spend time solemnly reflecting on my heart because I saw myself as a rule follower. I tended to consider myself more righteous than most. However, I took advantage of the law and looked for loopholes. My heart was not seeking God but instead following my own idea of how to live. Like the people preparing for the Sabbath as they hunted for all the leaven in the household to remove it, we too should scour our hearts and seek God without loopholes. Ask Him to turn your old water jars into his finest wine. God desires to make us new and changed into the best we were created to be.

Out with the Old, In with the New

> *Jesus answered, "I am the way and the truth and the life. No*
> *one comes to the Father except through me."*
> *(John 14:6)*

Jesus is perfectly clear: The old way and its principles of cleaning are over. The old way of sacrifices has also been done away with. There is a new way to holiness now. The road to redemption begins and ends at the cross. Out with the old; ring in the new.

> *These people come near to me with their mouth and honor me*
> *with their lips, but their hearts are far from me. Their worship*
> *of me is based on merely human rules they have been taught.*
> *(Isaiah 29:13)*

You cannot avoid Jesus and receive the benefits of eternal life. You must go through him to receive it. He is the way. God watched people act out rituals over and over to convey their holiness before crowds of men and to earn their own self-gratification. God listened to enough empty words spoken to him while the speaker's heart was far from him.

The six water jars were used for ceremonial cleaning. Jesus changed their use from cleansing jars to that which held the best wine. Jesus can change you in the same way. Will you allow him to?

The six jars were over in the corner. These jars were used for the Jewish rites of purification. Maybe they were old, chipped, and a bit dusty. Why six jars? Maybe those six jars symbolize man's efforts, his six days of labor. Jesus is taking what we would consider work, rules to live by, and turning them into a celebration. Is he trying to tell us that our redemption has nothing to do with our efforts? The six jars were changed and filled with his mercy and grace for the bride and groom.

Where, then, is boasting? It is excluded. Because of what law? The law that requires works? No, because of the law that requires faith.
(Romans 3:27)

We are no longer tied up with rules to keep us pure. Jesus changed the water into wine; this symbolizes many things. It reiterates that the cleansing traditions or manmade rules of work cannot be calculated into the work of the cross.

".....The Lord does not look at the things people look at. People look at the outward appearance, but the Lord looks at the heart."
(1 Samuel 16:7b)

For it is by grace you have been saved, through faith, and this is not from yourselves, it is the gift of God-not by works, so that no one can boast.
(Ephesians 2:8–9)

The Living Water and the Samaritan Woman

He said to me: "It is done. I am the Alpha and the Omega, the Beginning and the End. To the thirsty I will give water without cost from the spring of the water of life."
(Revelation 21:6)

In John 4, Jesus meets a Samaritan woman at the well. He asks her for a drink. Her response is, "You are a Jew and I a Samaritan woman. How can you ask me for a drink?" (v. 9). Here Jesus is breaking all the manmade rules again because God's new order for redemption is not ordered by race or status. The rules of the culture do not apply. Jesus went to Samaria to address her heart and her need for the living water. What cultural barriers does Jesus need to break through to reach you? He answers her, "If you knew the gift of God and who it is that asks you for a drink, you would have asked him and he would have given you Living Water."

Why does Jesus ignore her statement? Because he is always looking at our hearts.

> ".....acknowledge the God of your father, and serve him with wholehearted devotion and with a willing mind, for the Lord searches every heart and understands every desire and every thought. If you seek him, he will be found by you; but if you forsake him, he will reject you forever."
> (1 Chronicles 28:9)

Jesus knew everything about the Samaritan woman. He knew her past, her present, and her needs. He knew she needed the gift of God. He knows your needs. He knew that if she knew what he was offering her, the living water, she would have asked for it right away. Jesus defines the living water in verse 13: "Jesus answered, 'Everyone who drinks this water will be thirsty again, but whoever drinks the water I give him will never thirst. Indeed, the water I give him become in him a spring of water welling up to eternal life."

Jesus is using the metaphor of water to offer these promises: never be thirsty again; there is a spring of water welling up to eternal life. God uses water over and over to lead us, heal us, provide for us, and illustrate eternal life. He does this because he is the only one who can satisfy your deepest need. And as you taste it, it will be like drinking a living water.

When I turned to know Jesus, I had a vision. I was crawling across the desert, looking for water. Finally, I came over a hill and looked down to see an oasis of water. Once I reached the edge, I drank from it. I said to myself, "I have been thirsty for so long." I had no reference to the scripture supporting this, but I experienced it nonetheless. Later, as I read and studied the Word of God and learned about the living water, I was further touched by the truth of the Word of God!

Jesus reveals the condition of the Samaritan woman's heart by asking her for her husband and revealing that he knows how many husbands she has had. Her eyes are open, and she sees his power. She declares him a prophet. From there, he teaches her and defines worship.

"Yet a time is coming and has now come when the true worshipers will worship the Father in the Spirit and in truth, for they are the kind of worshipers the Father seeks. God is spirit, and his worshipers must worship in the Spirit and in truth." (John 4:23-24)

Remember the end of the story about the Wedding of Cana? The water leads us to the revealed truth of God. In John 2:11, it reads, "He thus revealed his glory, and his disciples put their faith in him." As they saw him change the water into wine, they saw his glory. They saw the God who rules over water and the elements of this world. The God who is gracious and humble came to cover the bride and groom's shame at the wedding. This Samaritan woman at the well saw the condition of her heart through the eyes of God. He did not judge her or shame her, but instead offered her eternal life and living water.

The woman said, "I know that Messiah" (called Christ) "is coming. When he comes, he will explain everything to us." Then Jesus declared, "I, the one speaking to you— I am he." (John 4:25-26)

Magnificent! Jesus reveals that he is the Messiah to a woman who was outcast by society and whose life resembled that of a prostitute. What I love most is this woman and many other women were elevated out of the cultural limitation and their hopeless lives to be given the greatest news anyone would ever desire. Halleluiah! Jesus brought the living water to a woman at the well. She was a Samaritan and a sinner. He breaks the cultural barriers and reaches us all. The Holy Spirit is hovering over the water!

The Vine

"I am the true vine …" (John 15:1)

The vineyard of the Lord Almighty is the nation of Israel, and the people of Judah are the vines he delighted in. And he

looked for justice, but saw bloodshed; for righteousness, but heard cries of distress.
(Isaiah 5:7)

You transplanted a vine from Egypt; you drove out the nations and planted it.
(Psalm 80:8)

This is my blood of the covenant, which is poured out for many for the forgiveness of sins. I tell you, I will not drink of this fruit of the vine from now on until that day when I drink it new with you in my Father's kingdom."
(Matthew 26:28-29)

So, my brothers and sisters, you also died to the law through the body of Christ, that you might belong to another, to him who was raised from the dead, in order that we might bear fruit for God. For when we were in the realm of the flesh, the sinful passions aroused by the law were at work in us, so that we bore fruit for death.
(Romans 7:4-5)

Do you see how the scripture connects God calling Israel a vine? It speaks of the drinking of the fruit of the vine and his blood covenant, which is remembered at the Last Supper. The thread of the blood covenant with mankind is consistent through the Word of God.

The Jewish nation is tied to the concept of wine at the wedding ceremony. Jesus does his first miracle at a wedding. I believe this was his announcement to all, that Jesus, the God of Israel and of all nations, is here. The bridegroom is seeking his bride. The changing of the water to wine represents the new way through Jesus. The sacrifices like the wine at the wedding ceremony, ran out. All the sacrifices of the Old Testament were temporary; they ran out. People needed a permanent remedy.

He is the atoning sacrifice for our sins, and not only for ours
but also for the sins of the whole world.
(1 John 2:2)

It is at the wedding ceremony with his first miracle Jesus reveals that he is God and he has come to make a new covenant with us. His glory revealed. He is announcing his purpose at this wedding ceremony in a quiet way.

But to those who were watching, the disciples, they saw God. They saw his glory. Did they know that a new covenant was coming, as foretold in Jeremiah 31:31–34?

> *"The days are coming," declares the Lord, "when I will make a new covenant with the people of Israel and with the people of Judah. It will not be like the covenant I made with their ancestors when I took them by the hand to lead them out of Egypt, because they broke my covenant, though I was a husband to them," declares the Lord. "This is the covenant I will make with the people of Israel after that time," declares the Lord. "I will put my law in their minds and write it on their hearts. I will be their God, and they will be my people. No longer will they teach their neighbor, or say to one another, 'Know the Lord,' because they will all know me, from the least of them to the greatest," declares the Lord. "For I will forgive their wickedness and will remember their sins no more."*
> *(Jeremiah 31:31-34)*

Are you ready to have your sins removed? My heart is touched with the love of God when I think about the verse above. God makes a lot of covenant promises to the house of Israel. The last statement is that he will forgive their wickedness and not remember their transgressions. Isn't it amazing? For us we have a holy God that plans to forget all our sins once we enter the covenant with him. That is a gift and a lifting of a burden. It is wiping away grime, cleansing us of sin, and giving us new hearts. This was his plan for mankind from the beginning, from the garden to this new covenant.

Here are some of the layers, like a layered wedding cake, lined up by point:

1. Israel is the vineyard.
2. The covenant of Abraham was a blood covenant.
3. The sacrifices of the old covenant were done with blood to cover mankind's sins. These were temporary.
4. Jesus changed the water into wine.
5. The tradition was for the best wine first, but Jesus gave the best wine last.
6. At the Last Supper, Jesus said, "This cup is the New Covenant in my blood, which is poured out for you."
7. We are to bear more fruit in living a life for God.

A Very Large Vine

Years ago, I lived in England, south of London. I had a yearly pass to the Palace of Henry the Eight. I loved to drive up there in the morning, push my daughter, Sophie, in her stroller over the cobblestone streets, and visit the palace and gardens. One of the most amazing sites was an old grape vine. This grape vine had grown so large that a glass house was built around it. A rope protected it so tourists couldn't walk under it. Yes, this vine was so large that one could walk underneath it. At the time, I believe the vine was about 250 years old. It was still producing grapes, which were used to make jam. Ever since viewing that grape vine, my sense of God's imagery concerning the vineyard has been enlarged. Can you imagine walking through a vineyard in which all the vines were this large?

The Garden

> *Father, if you are willing, take this cup from me, yet not my will, but yours be done.*
> *(Luke 22:42)*

Most of us are familiar with the third chapter of Genesis, when Adam and Eve walked with God in the garden. They had total freedom to access all of creation except one tree. They had total access to God also, but the temptation of sin bore into their flesh. Sin cast them out of the garden and away from God. Sin took full form, and murder shot out the gate within the first generation of children, in Cain and Abel. Between these two gardens, sin ravaged mankind, and the story is what I call "the messy middle." Sin is messy. Mankind is in a mess. There is only one remedy, and that is Jesus. Fast forward to the end of Jesus's life, and it is in a garden. In the Garden of Gethsemane, Jesus sweats blood as he thinks about all of mankind's sins being laid upon him and the agony he will soon face at the cross. The consequences of the Garden of Eden are transported to Christ. On the cross he acquires our sentence as he accepts the will of his Father.

As I have said earlier, sin separates us from God. Due to their sin, Adam and Eve were cast out of the Garden of Eden and no longer walk with God. Jesus took on the sins of the world, knowing that in addition to the pain of suffering of the crucifixion, the pain of being separated from his Father would be unbearable.

Jesus was in prayer to his Father, and he asked, "Father, if you are willing, take this cup from me."

We cannot get away from the reference of the cup, as he is praying to sustain himself for what is ahead. This verse brings it all together. He is being poured out for us, a living sacrifice. I don't want my words to get in the way here. Think about how this lines up together so seamlessly.

I cannot help but think about when we are facing something we dread, this is how we should pray. You should ask God to remove it, but if it is his will, ask him to sustain you through the difficult time. Jesus shows his humanity and his humility as he asks to not have to suffer the cross.

> *And when the sixth hour had come, there was darkness over the whole land until the ninth hour. And at the ninth hour Jesus cried with a loud voice, "Eloi, Eloi, lema sabachthani?" which means, "My God, my God, why have you forsaken me?" (Mark 15:33–34)*

The ugliness of our sins laid upon Jesus, so his Father would not look upon his face. He turned from his son. Father and son separated because of us, by the sins of mankind. While the pain of the cross was horrendous, being separated from his Father was horrendous. Just a few verses later, he dies. As I hear Jesus words, he calls out to his Father, "My God, My God, why have you forsaken me," That was my sin, your sin, our sin that separated a father and son and crushed Jesus.

Jesus took our sorrows to his death, but the added sorrow of being separated from his Father pained him as well. He cried out for his Father as he suffered. And because of the ugliness of mankind's sin, his Father could not look upon the son whom "he loved and was well pleased."

The temple veil was torn; the sacrifice was complete. Now Jesus is our high priest, who gives us a full-access pass to God and the kingdom of heaven. Remember that the veil signifies we are set aside, symbolic of an intimate relationship for one who chose us. My friend, God has chosen you. He has removed the veil so that you may draw close to him—so that you may know him. This is the new way.

Remember the invitation at the beginning of the book? Remember Jesus's words, "Come follow me"? He calls the nation of Israel, and he is calling all of mankind individually. He wants you. He wants you to know him intimately. The veil is gone. He is here, as close as your breath.

Remain in Me

In the book of John, the phrase "remain in" is repeated several times.

> Remain in me, as I also remain in you. No branch can bear
> fruit by itself; it must remain in the vine. Neither can you
> bear fruit unless you remain in me. "I am the vine; you are
> the branches. If you remain in me and I in you, you will bear
> much fruit; apart from me you can do nothing."
> (John 15:4-5)

Lastly, it tells us to "remain in the vine." Meditate upon all that you know. From start to finish, the Bible reveals Jesus and his plan to redeem us. "Remain in the vine" is a command that has depth. It is what we consider as we have communion with God, partaking in the bread and wine offered up in remembrance. Consider all that he has laid out, from the beginning to the end. All of this is done to bring us to the perfect ending of eternal life with him as his children.

Communion brings us the table of Christ: his love, his blood shed for us, the completeness of his sacrifice.

We are connected to God, attached as a branch is attached to the vine. If we draw close to him, we are going to bear fruit. The fruit of God will spill out of us into the lives of others. Why wouldn't you want to spill forth more love, peace, joy, forbearance, goodness, faithfulness, gentleness, and self-control?

As this is a book concerning the topic of marriage, we must compare our relationship with our spouse to our relationship with God. I can offer this simple guideline.

1. Draw close to God.
2. Love one another.

Of course, we know where this idea is from.

> *Jesus replied: "'Love the Lord your God with all your heart and with all your soul and with all your mind.' This is the first and greatest commandment. And the second is like it: "Love your neighbor as yourself."*
> *(Matthew 22:37-39)*

Jesus made it simple. These two verses cover it all.

The Bookends of Two Celebrations
The Moving Jar

The Wedding of Cana and the Last Supper are like bookends for Jesus's ministry before he began the work of the cross. During both events, he shared a meal with friends. During both meals, wine played a significant role. At the Last Supper, he asked us to remember his sacrifice with the cup of wine. He celebrated the fulfillment of a covenant with mankind.

This is the reception banquet, the time where we are to celebrate mankind being redeemed. He wants us to continue to celebrate this even now. Of course, we do this through Easter and Holy Communion. But we can also do this through prayer as we thank him for all he has done and will do for us.

There is one more thing that these two events have in common: water jars.

> *Nearby stood six stone water jars, the kind used by the Jews for ceremonial washing, each holding from twenty to thirty gallons.*
> *(John 2:6)*

> *Jesus sent Peter and John saying, "Go and make preparations for us to eat the Passover." "Where do you want us to prepare for it?" they asked. He replied, "As you enter the city, a man carrying a jar of water will meet you, follow him to the house he enters."*
> *(Luke 22:8–10)*

This last jar, the seventh jar, leads them to the Last Supper. Perhaps, the seventh jar symbolizes the work done by Jesus on the cross, and we are now to rest in him, just like the Sabbath Day of rest. This last jar leads us to the house Jesus enters! Notice the first six jars at the Wedding of Cana are stagnant, and this last jar is moving. Remember, the six jars were the cleansing jars. For those, the Jewish leaders made extensive laws that were burdensome and required man to work hard to demonstrate his outward holiness. The seventh jar, the Passover jar, is moving. It is leading them to the place of the Last Supper and to the house where Jesus entered. Jesus asked Peter and John to follow it as it led them to the covenant supper, the Last Supper. Jesus is the living water, the water that changes us from sinners to the redeemed! Are you going to follow it? Take one last look at the end of the scripture in Luke 22. Jesus tells them to follow the man carrying the water jar—follow him to the house he enters.

At the wedding, the bridegroom invites the bride into the huppah. We have learned over and over that God pursues us to live with him in his kingdom for all eternity. Jesus continually asks man to follow him, seek him, and remain in him. In John 14, he offers comfort to the disciples at the Last Supper after he has told them that he is going to lay down his life for them. These are the words of comfort:

> *"Do not let your hearts be troubled. You believe in God; believe also in me. My Father's house has many rooms; if that were not so, would I have told you that I am going there to prepare a place for you? And if I go and prepare a place for you, I will come back and take you to be with me that you also may be where I am."*
> *(John 14: 1-3)*

He is building you a dwelling place. How cool is this? Accept the invitation to follow Christ. Follow Him!

The significance of the wine goes further. Jesus has made a promise not to drink again of the fruit of the vine until the fulfillment of the kingdom of God. He is fasting from the fruit of the vine until we are with him in his kingdom. This is just more and more significant. It truly is amazing how much meaning this all has.

> *Then he took a cup, and when he had given thanks, he gave it to them, saying, "Drink from it, all of you. This is my blood of the covenant, which is poured out for many for the forgiveness of sins. I tell you, I will not drink from this fruit*

of the vine from now on until that day when I drink it new
with you in my Father's kingdom."
(Matthew 26:27-29)

He is waiting for us, to hold a banquet in our honor. You can be sure the wine will be significant at this celebration.

Chapter 11 Questions

1. How do your ideas of purity and communion with God tie together?

2. How have your thoughts on communion changed?

3. What are some ways to remain in Christ?

4. Does the story of the wedding of Cana have any more significance to you?

12

The Banquet

"After that, we who are still alive and are left will be caught up together with them in the clouds to meet the Lord in the air. And so we will be with the Lord forever."
(1 Thessalonians 4:17)

"My Father's house has many rooms; if that were not so, would I have told you that I am going there to prepare a place for you? And if I go and prepare a place for you, I will come back and take you to be with me that you also may be where I am. You know the way to the place where I am going."
(John 14:2-4)

In our limited capacity we try to imagine the banquet. It brings us a joyous anticipation. But we know our mind really cannot phantom how beautiful it will be.

A Banquet Story

In my imagination I am leaning against glass looking into a beautiful room, an enormous banquet. Long tables set about the room with the finest linens, topped with beautiful place settings of clay and gold. The front of the room was filled with a long row of magnificent thrones. On a few of the thrones were seated glorious kings, while more kings walked in taking their places. The room was adorned with tapestries and flaming candelabras. Musicians strolled about in harmony weaving between the conversation of the crowds. Taking a quick glance at the gate, I saw many people entering. I knew who each person was. As they passed, they greeted me as a friend. Every person was wearing a crown. In stunned amazement I stood for the longest time, watching as the crowd gathered. As they passed by me, I understood their place and time here on earth. There was Jonah walking with ancient people from across all the nations and time. Next came former presidents, diplomats, and kings, listening to stories of this young man whom in his former life could not speak or walk. Queen Esther stood talking with my fourth-grade teacher as if they had known one another forever.

My eyes feasted on the nations of people. Their beauty blending with seamless harmony. They were friends, at ease with one another, no boundary lines between them. Not just mere friends, but more. There was this love flowing between all the people, those who previously had strife with one another, their countries in constant war. I saw more people whom had suffered greatly and served with no reward. King David walked in with shop keepers from China. The poorest of the poor from third world countries continued to flow past me. Many people from all nations and all time continued to be added. The beauty overwhelmed me. The mingling of those from Biblical times with those who looked like neighbors drew me to breathe deep. Their life stories became knowledge to me, laid upon my heart. People from concentration camps, prisons, tribes across the world walking and talking with one another. Everyone was friends. I saw my sister across the room and she gave me the most beautiful smile. I saw Abraham talking with a young man who was killed in a terrible war. I saw Peter and the thief on the cross. I saw Noah and the woman who gave her last penny to the temple talking with shoe shiners from Bolivia.

A vast number of people, gentle and kind walked through the gate. One woman was from America. She lived a shallow life of self-indulgence. But her countenance said she was no longer the same person. A well-known preacher walked in with a tribe of people from the Amazon forest. People from the beginning of time and all through the centuries came in. There were former shepherds, car mechanics, beauticians, tent makers, mothers of lost children, soldiers, martyrs, people that had suffered great diseases, famine, torture, and prejudice. Former slaves, abandoned children, and those who had never learned to read or write accepted the invitation of this celebration. Those who were terribly abused, neglected, never loved, never wanted looked whole and at peace.

There was something so familiar and familial amongst them. It was a love, a completeness, a recognition that they were family, all counted the same. They seemed to have love and joy, sincerely cherishing this bond with one another. The excitement was too much. I wanted in. I did not want to miss this banquet.

I noticed in the front of the room was the most glorious King of all Kings. He was so bright and beautiful. He kept looking at me. His eyes were piercing, full of love and knowledge, pulling me into the room, toward him. I am not sure what I was waiting for. Then the next person that passed me was from the Book of Luke, the prodigal son. As he passed me, he stopped, turned around, and waved me into the banquet. He asked, "What are you waiting for?"

I stepped into the room. As I looked down at my feet I noticed I was wearing a beautiful robe. My body felt different; lighter and tighter, less wobbly than it started to feel in days past. A different feeling broke out on the inside. My mind was set right. My heart contained only the good it was intended to hold from the beginning of time. I felt so right; so complete! As I stepped forward, a blanket of warmth enveloped me, as if I were in a different atmosphere. I looked to the first people in front of me. They knew me, my life story, my name. Then love took residence between us. We conversed, I moved on to the next new friends. It was Apostle Paul and a mix of people who welcomed me again with love and knowledge of my life story.

Drawing forward, it was the greatest event I had ever attended. I wondered how did I get invited? How did I get on the list for such an invitation? How was I accepted to dine with such people of history, sacrifice, and love? A magnetic gravitational pull led me to his presence. There, I stood before the greatest of all, King and Savior Jesus. I fell. Fell to the ground before him.

Time was no longer here to measure. During a very long moment, I was brought to a new plane of knowledge of myself, understanding what this King Jesus wanted for me, how he had created me, how he knew everything about me, loved me, and shed his blood for me. I came to full knowledge of him. I continued to gain understanding responding with an openness of adoration and thanksgiving. Again, how long I lay before him could not be recorded in earthly time. Finally, someone gently lifted me. I did not want to leave. Looking into King Jesus's eyes gave me a reassurance, a peace. I understood that I was secure. I was here to stay with him and these new people, my new family. Then I said to myself, "I am home. I am finally home." I felt a weight settle upon my head. I reached up, touched what seemed to be a crown. Turning, I moved around the room meeting more new friends. They all called me sister. I shared with them what had happened when I met the King. They all shook their heads in understanding. They too had bowed before him.

As time went on, I started to realize this was my new family, and I was overwhelmed. So many, yet it felt so intimate. And I kept repeating to myself, "I am home. I am finally home."

Welcome Home

"….when we've been there ten thousand years…"

> *"And night will be no more. They will need no light of lamp or sun, for the Lord God will be their light, and they will reign forever and ever."*
> *(Revelation 22:5)*

> *"Consequently, he is able to save to the uttermost those who draw near to God through him, since he always lives to make intercession for them."*
> *(Hebrews 7:25)*

Have you considered the greetings we will speak to one another once we are transformed and transported to our heavenly home? Good morning! But there is no night. Have a great day! But there is no sorrow. How are you? Only peace and joy reign. What have you been up to? I have been living with Jesus the last ten thousand years. What's new? I have been meeting my new brother and sisters from all around the globe and time!

Maybe our greeting will be, "Welcome home." Because I believe there will be an unending, inwardly thankfulness with deep appreciation we made it home to Jesus! Welcome home! I am so glad I am home, finally home! Thank you, Jesus!

Just another day in heaven, I look forward to sitting in the warmth of God's light, wading into the waters knee deep alongside a new sister or brother with Jesus at our side. This new friend maybe from the Marshall Islands; Somalia; Canada; Papua New Guinea; Sri Lanka; Libya; Israel or so on.

We greet one another, "Welcome home!" The sharing starts. Please tell me the moment you met Jesus and your story was birthed?

So the story begins:

I was sitting in the hospital. I slipped down a mountain. I was praying for God to show me who He is. The lyrics of a song touched me. It was during the war. I just buried my child. I was in jail for murder. I looked in the mirror at myself. I grew up on the streets with no family. My daughter asked me if I believed in God. I heard myself say I wanted to end my life. My husband left me. I had a dream about Jesus. Someone fed me and shared Jesus. I had so many addictions. My daddy taught me about Jesus. I grew up with great fear and depression. I was overwhelmed with the feeling I was not perfect, a sinner. I watched the sun set over the mountains. All day I worked to feed my family a small bowl of food. I was abandoned. I lived with constant war. My neighbor was so kind to me. I felt so alone. A friend shared the love of Jesus and his dying on the cross for me. I was reading the Word of God.

Each story so beautiful displaying the vastness of God's power intervening upon a man's hard, hurting, despicable heart. He renders his love, compassion, forgiveness and mercy upon our stony life of rebellion and sorrow. Taking each of us from time and place into his glorious presence. Rescuing us from ourselves!

Then Jesus speaks. He shares, "I remember when I went before the throne of My Father, holding the cup I shed for you, asking him to turn his eyes toward you… As you sat in the dark of night crying and broken….when you were violated… when a friend told a horrible rumor about you… when people laughed at the way you looked…when the soldiers came into your village and stole you from your family…when you got rid of that baby growing inside of you…when you broke your marriage vows….when you got the horrible news of an illness…when your loved one died… when you lost your job…when you laid in the street after a bomb landed twenty feet from you…when you realized you did something horrible, unforgiveable… when you wasted the precious gift of time doing nothing."

"You thought you were alone, unlovable. You listened to lies; you were not important, a loser. No one would notice if you were gone. You had no purpose. You were so overwhelmed with anger you felt out of control. The hurt was so deep you wanted to be numb. You had no one who loved you. Life was empty."

"Then I touched you. You were healed. Your heart was changed from a stony briquette to a heart of flesh. You were lifted from a pit of fire into my presence. I made you a new creation. I adopted you into my family. I anointed you with oil. I placed you in the palm of my hand and covered you."

"Then one glorious day I called you home. No more separation between us. I wanted us to meet face to face. I know your desire, yearning to look in my eyes, to feel the strength and warmth of my embrace. Your unquenchable desire to hear my voice, to touch my wounds of afflictions. To know me wholly, to worship me in nearness."

"So welcome home my child! I have been waiting for this day since before the creation of the world. The day we would meet face to face. Welcome home!"

My friend, this book has come to an end. I hope to meet you at the banquet. You will know who I am. I will be the one who shouts: "Welcome home!"

Chapter 12 Questions

1.   Do you believe that Christ has created a beautiful ending for you?

2.   How do you feel about being called the bride of Christ?

3.   What have you learned from this book that increased or changed your faith?

End Notes,

Helen Latner, *Your Jewish Wedding*, Doubleday and Company, Inc. Garden City, New York 1985

Jamie Lashm, *The Ancient Jewish Wedding*, Jewish Jewels, Ft. Lauderdale, Fl., 1997

Anita Diamant, *The New Jewish Wedding*, Simon and Schuster, 1985

Michael Asheri, *Living Jewish*, Everest House Publishers, 1978

Helen Latner, *The Everything Jewish Wedding Book*, Adam Media Corporation, Avon, Massachusetts, 1998

Rabbi Solomon Ganzfried, *Code of Jewish Law*, Hebrew Publishing Company, New York, 1961, 1963

Rabbi Benjamin Blech, *Understanding Judaism*, Penguin Group, New York, New York, 2003

Ronald L. Eisenberg, *JPS Guide Jewish Traditions*, The Hewish Publication Society, Philadelphia, Penn. 2008

John J. Parsons, *Wedding Blessings-Sheva Berachot*, http://www.hebrew4christians.com/Blessings/Special_Events/Wedding_Blessings/wedding., 2015

Henri J. M. Nouwen, *The Return of the Prodigal Son*, Image Books, Doubleday, New York, New York, 1994

Printed in the United States
By Bookmasters